GUIDELINES FOR
CONTEMPORARY CATHOLICS:
Penance and Reconciliation

GUIDELINES FOR CONTEMPORARY CATHOLICS:
Penance and Reconciliation

Patrick J. Brennan

THE THOMAS MORE PRESS
Chicago, Illinois

ISBN 0-88347-195-7

CONTENTS

Discussion questions and a
list of suggested readings
follow each chapter

To Heather,
who teaches me a great deal
about love and forgiveness.

Publication of this book
is made possible in part
by a grant from
ANDREW M. GREELEY

INTRODUCTION

PENANCE and reconciliation are values and practices deeply rooted in the Judaeo-Christian tradition. If they are not looked at, talked about, and prayed over by believers of the present age, their importance for us may be lost. Penance and reconciliation need to be looked at anew and reinterpreted for contemporary Catholics. That is the purpose of this study. Too often penance and reconciliation are looked on by many Catholics as superstitious practices of the spiritually immature, or crutches needed by the neurotically guilt-ridden. In such generalizing, Catholic Christians are losing touch with a crucial dimension of conversion spirituality and our tradition. Reinterpreting the practice of penance and reconciliation and suggesting paths of future development will necessitate two other movements in this book: an analysis of these phenomena in current American Catholic culture and a study of the historical evolution of the sacrament. I sincerely hope that these and other parts of the book are helpful for individual and/or group study.

Patrick Brennan

Chapter One

CONFUSED SACRAMENT, MUDDLED CONSCIENCES

An American Invasion of Ireland?

"YOU Americans are invading us," the young man said. He was a slender young man, about sixteen years of age. Our conversation took place in a small town in central Ireland. I was driving through on my way to a speaking engagement in the eastern section of the country. He was an attendant at a service station where I had stopped for gas.

"Oh?" I reacted. "Are a lot of Americans here this summer?" "Yes!" he exclaimed with both exasperation and enthusiasm. I drove off, but the boy's words remained with me: "You Americans are invading us." At first I had heard only the literal content: a comment about travel and vacations. As I drove down Ireland's narrow streets, however, another message began to resonate within me.

"You Americans are invading us!" If the numbers of vacationing Americans had increased in this part of Europe, there must have also been a growth in the influence of American values in Ireland. From the time of that conversation with the young man, I began to notice more attentively the people of this land of my roots. I saw a beautifully simple and good people seemingly at war, in conflict. The essence of the conflict is Irish tradition vs. American consumerism. Everywhere I traveled in Ireland the gentle beauty and simplicity of Irish song and dance was being raped by the harshness of rock music and American style advertising.

"You Americans are invading us!" "We are," I privately lamented. If only the issue was the number of travelers. The greater crisis, Ireland and wherever else capitalism has had an influence, is the diminishing of person-centered, God-centered values and the expansion of the empty values of consumerism.

Listen To The Words

Irish young people, like American young people, walk down the streets with portable stereos in hand. The units blare with melodies whose words I rarely attend to. A recent editorial in *Newsweek* magazine, however, has sensitized me to the issue of words in rock songs. The editorial was written by a journalist-mother, in her late thirties. The woman confessed to being a fan of rock music, having grown up with it as a staple of American culture. The point of her writing, however, was anchored in moral concern. She had taken to listening to the words of contemporary rock. One hit by a well-known female vocalist sang of the feelings a woman experienced upon the penetration of her vagina by a man's penis. Another by a top male vocalist told in folksy style of a young woman masturbating with a newspaper. Still another artist was quoted by the mother-journalist as adorning herself with crucifixes because she liked the feel of a naked male body, even if in miniature and in the form of a religious symbol.

The mother reported a certain guilt over her own naiveté. She had no idea that her children were listening to such sexually explicit lyrics. Her purpose in writing was not so much the moral judgment of any of the individual acts mentioned above. She was concerned, rather, that music has a formative effect on young people's imaginations. Were her children, she wondered, subconsciously being manipulated by rock music toward sexual activity. Her second concern was that all of this was going on in her world, in her home, and she had given little attention to it. She closed the article by encouraging parents to pay closer heed to the media's influence on young people.

Asleep at the Switch?

The article impressed me because it pointed to what I believe to be the condition of morality in America today: one of widespread desensitization. There are so many aspects of daily life in America to which we do not pay attention; we almost seem anesthestized to them. Besides the wary mother's concern over the frequently ignored sexually explicit lyrics of songs, there's the en masse manipulation of people through advertising, the use of children to sell products, television violence that suggests to viewers that what is obviously destructive behavior will not maim or injure people, sexism and the use of eroticism for advertising, and racism. All the while nuclear arms proliferate at an alarming rate, and the ordinary citizen knows little either about their production or destructive ability. Someone else will take care of defense and the control of nuclear arms for us, we think. In a similarly alienating, estranging pattern, professionals of various sorts—from teachers, to doctors, to counselors—have assumed some of the natural functions and roles of the nuclear family, resulting in what psychologist David Elkind calls "the patchwork" young person—children who move into adolescence with identities "scotch taped" together rather than growing integrally from within. So many of the patterns and practices of contemporary Western society are dehumanizing, alienating, and estranging. But we have grown conditioned to not look, to not see, to not hear, to not pay attention.

A Current Cultural Reflection
of Ancient Scriptural Wisdom

Our culturally conditioned desensitization has infiltrated
our sense of evil and sin. This ought not to be too surpris-
ing, for Scripture frequently portrays sin as essentially
subtle, a force that, in effect, creeps up on us, in us, and
around us without our paying much attention to it. Chap-
ters 3–11 of Genesis portray sin as essentially attitudinal,
incarnated in intangible yet real forces like greed, lust, re-
sentment, ambition, idolatry and an often unarticulated
feeling that one can go it alone without God. As we turn
the pages of Scripture from the early mythic literature that
also contains the seeds of Judaeo-Christian faith, we move
into the historical accounts of the developing nation Israel.
Sin is often reported to be a lack of remembering, a not
paying attention. Israel had a tendency to forget God and
the covenant bond that it had as a nation with Yahweh.
The Old Testament says that it is a subtly hurtful spirit or
attitude and a malaise of attentiveness or consciousness
that gradually leads to hurtful or destructive behavior. In
our secularized age, where the counselor frequently takes
on the previously sacralized role of priest, or holy person,
the counselor often deals in the same categories of problematic attitudes that lead to hurtful or destructive
behavior. Psychotherapy can serve as a modern analog or
reflection of the conversion therapy encouraged by the Old
Testament: change your heart; change your behavior.

The Poetic Simplicity of the Psalms

The psalms poetically capture the Old Testament attitudes towards sin. Psalm 12 refers to "a double heart"
that leads to a life of falsehood. Psalm 14 says that some

people foolishly say in their hearts that there is no God, and that such "heart stances" lead to corrupt behavior. In the 32nd psalm, the author speaks of the human spirit as a force that needs a "bit and bridle," like a horse or mule, to curb the will. The 36th psalm locates sin "in the depths of the heart," and speaks of the sinner as someone who has "turned his back on wisdom." In Psalm 37, we read of interior anger and rage that leads in turn to drawing the sword and bending the bow. The 50th psalm warns against "detesting discipline." The classic penitential psalm, Psalm 51, beautifully speaks of God as the only source of cleansing and healing from sin and reminds penitents that not empty religious practices, but a contrite heart is the proper sacrifice that both turns a lifestyle around from sinful attitudes and ways and also appeases God.

The Expansive View of the Prophets

Though the psalms interpret what some might call "dark nights of the soul," or times when God seems distant from the people, as God forgetting Israel (see Psalm 44), more often the Scriptures suggest that sin is rather the people forgetting God. Individual forgetting compounds itself into collective forgetting. Thus the nation Israel would move into periods of collective estrangement from God. The prophets, especially, speak of this "corporate sin." The first author of Isaiah (Isaiah appears to be really three treatises edited into one) begins the book by addressing a "sinful nation, a people weighed down with guilt. . . . who have turned away" (from God) (1:4). God, through Jeremiah, speaks to a nation that has "abandoned me . . . the fountain of living water. . . . and prostituted (itself) with many lovers" (2:13; 3:2). Ezechiel speaks of the House of Israel, which "enshrines idols . . . in (the) heart." This

idolatry of the heart leads Yahweh to "reduce the country
to desert . . . and punish their faithlessness to me" (14:3;
15:8).

Whether individual or corporate, sin in the Old Testament is a marriage between attitude and behavior.

Along Comes Jesus

One of the key conflicts between Jesus and the scribes
and Pharisees was over *sin*—sometimes the word is not
clearly spoken, but it is obvious what is at issue is sin, or
evil. The Jewish leaders of Jesus' age had contrived for
themselves and others an interesting system of what we
might call "churchy" morality and sin. In other words,
goodness or evil were often determined by adherence to the
norms and criteria of the bureaucracy or institution. With
its preoccupation with its religious, institutionalized criteria for discernment, many adherents of Judaism of the
time were increasingly blinded to the depth of their subtle
sin, both individually and collectively. Religion had become for many a way of ignoring the deeper afflictions of
the heart and lifestyle. As long as one could focus on the
heavily externalized moral code, he or she need not deal
with the idolatry, anger, or any one of a number of other
demonic forces lurking within which negatively affected
and caused discord in relationships. Both Matthew and
Luke depicted the inauguration of Jesus' ministry as a
wrestling with the subtle, intangible, but real forces of sin
as he confronted the possibilities of anchoring his life in
power, greed, and impulse.

In Matthew's twenty-third chapter, Jesus indicts the
Pharisees for their preoccupation with religious externals
and inattention to the interior nature of the human spirit.

Matthew's concept of sin is rounded out in Matthew 25, wherein reward or punishment at the end of life is depicted as depending on whether or not one is compassionate in behavior. The Lukan Jesus similarly speaks of sin as a tension between attitude and behavior in chapter six. "A man's words flow out of what fills his heart," Jesus teaches (6:45). "Love your enemies," he counsels in the same chapter, "be compassionate . . . give . . ." (6:27, 38). Moral integrity, for Jesus, is discerning God's will and acting on it (6:46). A more extensive discussion of moral discernment appears elsewhere in the book.

The scriptural portrait of Jesus, then, depicts a prophetic voice that recapitulates the moral teaching of the Old Testament: sin is subtle, attitudinal. Such attitudinal sin leads to sinful behavior. However, both then and now, sin is missed; not paid attention to. In fact, the trappings of religion can disguise sin, distract one from paying attention to it. As with psychotherapy today, moral therapy, in Christian terms, must be a marriage between attitudinal and behavior change. This brief survey of Scripture reiterates the theme begun under the discussion of changing Irish and American culture, that is, the gradual eroding power of evil in human nature.

The "More" of Jesus: A Revelation Through Heather

Jesus added to the Old Testament; he did not just restate it. Jesus ushered in a new ethic—the norm of love. What undergirds Christian morality is love. In a moment of closeness with my three-year-old niece, Heather, I asked her if she realized how much I loved her. Mischief and attention-getting gave way to a flash of sincerity on her face. Yes, she nodded; she realized how much her uncle

loved her. "How much is that?" I asked. She held up all of
her fingers and said, "This much!" Her childish use of
fingers to indicate maximum quantity was her way of saying that she intuited from me an unconditional love of her.
That three-year-old flash of intuition about familial love is
what the Kingdom preaching of Jesus sought to do: awaken
people to a love force in their lives, the force of God's
unconditional love for each individual. The revolutionary,
motivating dynamic for morality in the Christian vision is
no longer guilt or fear. These are at best impoverished versions of morality's true motivation: love. The person in
conversion to the Kingdom or Reign of God struggles to
live a moral life because of *responsibility that flows from
love.* Responsibility that flows from love is the result of a
good parenting or teaching style between an adult and a
child. Jesus revealed that such is to be the style of morality
in his new way. Disciples do "the good" for the same reason Heather and other children (sometimes) "do the
good." Love prompts moral action.

The Active, Unconditional Love
of God that Leads to Contrition

The Pharisees and scribes often challenged Jesus about
the type of people with whom he associated. These "obviously religious" men, not aware of their own moral fail-
ings, further blinded themselves by their dissociation from
certain types of people whom they labeled as "sinful."
Their religioned, institutionalized view of sin was that it
was a force "out there," removed from themselves, alive
in others. Yet the very people whom others condemned or
ostracized were the ones with whom Jesus associated.
Jesus' reaching out to sinners, those in questionable pro-

fessions, and the diseased whose afflictions were presumed to result from sin, was itself a parabolic statement. Parabolic stories as well as parabolic gestures in the gospels are often Jesus' way of revealing the nature of the God of mystery. The God of Jesus, with his unconditional love, actively pursues the sinful or alienated person. So much of Jesus' activity could be recast verbally into something like this: "Look at me. Do you see how I seek out the morally, physically, and emotionally broken! This is the way God our Father is." James Mackey, in his book *Jesus: The Man and the Myth,* says that one of the reasons the religious leadership wanted Jesus killed was that the God he preached was "close and available." Such a God was quite different from the god that they taught—a god of an apparent *Monopoly* game, who could only be reached with crafty moves, complicated strategies, and lots of setbacks.

The power of the love of God, flowing through the healing ministry of Jesus, changed people's lives. This is evidenced in multiple gospel accounts, like the story of Zacchaeus, the woman at the well, the woman caught in adultery, the man born blind, and many other stories of physical or interior healing. In these stories, God's active, unconditional love elicits a response of love, a new attitude of responsibility regarding the gift of life and relationships.

Theologians have referred to the phenomenon of love changing a sinful heart as *contrition.* Thomas Aquinas distinguished between contrition and attrition. Attrition refers to life change and sorrow for sin because of fear. Contrition, on the other hand, is prompted by love. As the sacrament, the incarnation of God's love, Jesus' healings prompted conversion. In some cases, as God's love came upon sin it elicited a unique dimension of conversion: contrition, sorrow rooted in love. Contrition is a primary stage in a process that leads to repentance and a turning toward God, often called *metanoia.*

An Example: Hot Words on a Sunday Morning

I often think of a Sunday morning when I was in that semirebellious period of preadolescence. I wanted to do something with friends, something that my mother would not permit. I reacted to her discipline with hostility, saying things that I should not have said, using language that was not appropriate for communication with one's mother. After the verbal exchange, I stalked out of the house—one of those pubescent walk-out scenes designed to frighten parents that the child might not return. But my anger abated quickly after I left the house. I knew within my own heart that I had over-reacted, had been uncompromising, had been at least verbally abusive. The interior discomfort was considerable. It was guilt, but it was genuine guilt. The guilt was not rooted in fear or obligation, for the essence of my mother's relationship to her children had been one of sacrificial love. I walked to my parish church which had a religious goods store off of the vestibule. Whatever money I had in my pocket was sufficient to purchase a small, glass-like statue of Mary, the mother of Jesus. I bought the statue and hurried home. With stumbling words and halting behavior, I offered the gift to my mother—an obvious attempt to say that I was sorry for my inappropriate words and behavior.

She immediately treasured the statue, since she was quite devoted to Mary. More importantly, for me, she hugged me and without any games accepted my repentance. Her forgiveness was rooted in her unconditional love. She knew "that I knew" that I had been unreasonable. My repentant action was obviously motivated by the love I knew that she had for me. Her acceptance of my repentance re-enforced my contrition.

Irish families, back in my childhood period, tended to parcel out responsibilities—which parent would be the disciplinarian, which would be the source of support. Recent research has, of course, encouraged the sharing of these two familial responsibilities by both mother and father. However, at least in my family, discipline seemed to fall to my father, and nurturance to my mother. Because of these polarities, my mother more often prompted something akin to contrition in me; whereas my father's firm hand prompted variations of attrition.

Cultural Catholicism's Strange Gods

Could it be that not enough Catholics (and Christians in general) yet believe in the God of Jesus, the God of unconditional love and forgiveness, the God who loves us into responsibility? Often we refashion God into our own images and thus miss the experience of the truly good news of God's love and forgiveness. Perhaps it is this guilt-producing, anxiety-raising God that is often consciously or unconsciously connected with the sacrament of reconciliation, thus making the sacrament something to be avoided, rather than pursued. Most people carry enough emotional or spiritual pain within them without adding to it with what is, in effect, a dysfunctional God image. The "burden of Jesus" is light. What he offers to the human family, individually and collectively, is the fullness of life that comes from oneness with God and solidarity with other human beings. It is this approach to God, Jesus, salvation, and reconciliation that the world is truly hungering for. It is unfortunate that the church puts such life-changing opportunities for reconciliation "under a bushel," in favor of nonscriptural approaches to God and an often alienating sacramental practice.

What the World Needs Now: Responsibility

"How can you say to your brother, 'Brother, let me take out the splinter that is in your eye; when you cannot see the plank in your own? Hypocrite! Take the plank out of your own eye first, and then you will see clearly enough to take out the splinter that is in your brother's eye." Jesus' challenge in the sixth chapter of Luke is an admonition to claim responsibility for one's own morality. Both Karl Menninger, in *Whatever Happened to Sin,* and M. Scott Peck, in *People of the Lie,* have written, not only about the subtle nature of sin which we spoke of earlier, but also the human tendency to deflect responsibility for sin and its consequences. Others sin, we feel. Sin is part of impersonal institutions and organizations. But we often think to ourselves, *my* sin is not significant.

The essence of morality is *responsibility*—responsibility for and with the gift of life. The responsibility extends to both one's individual life and the quality of life in general. As we lose sensitivity to responsibility for life and our own participation in the evil of the world, the quality of life subtly erodes. When we deflect moral sensitivity, there is, in effect, "no one minding the store." We expect someone else to improve the quality of life. We become blinded to our own sin and need for repentance. As we have abandoned, over the course of recent years, a preoccupation with sin and what moralists call "act morality" (that is, "the grocery list" approach to confession), perhaps we have "thrown the baby out with the bath water." Maybe we have begun to lose our sense of sin.

Contemporary language often euphemizes this moral blurring. Abortions are referred to as "terminating pregnancies." Promiscuity has become "heightened sexual activity." Potentially catastrophic nuclear build-up is "arms parity." Toxic patterns of relating, emoting, valuing, or communicating are "psychologized" away as the result of one's training, background, or familial environment. "How few look at their own consciences," Bishop Oscar Romero said one day before his assassination. "Today's world is a kind of anonymous world in which no one wants to take the blame. . . . We are all sinners. . . ." "Take care of the plank in your own eye," Jesus exclaims to the modern world. These words are an expression of a key piece of the vision of the Reign of God that Jesus revealed—vigilance. Kingdom people are vigilant about the quality of life, beginning with the quality of one's individual life.

Cheap Grace Sacraments

"Cheap grace" was a term used by Dietrich Bonhoeffer to critique the style of Christianity, worship, and sacraments that he saw operative in the Europe of the 1930s and 1940s. Bonhoeffer was troubled by the externalized style of religious practice. Catholics and Protestants alike were engaging in ritual, but the ritual seemed to be without significant life change. Toward the end of his life, Bonhoeffer began to rethink church as existing not in and for itself but rather for the transformation of the world. Sacraments that were not intimately related to personal conversion and to the transformation of culture and life were vehicles of cheap grace, in Bonhoeffer's view. Cheap grace, that is, ritual without religious experience, is no grace at all.

The religious educator Johannes Hofinger lamented the

"cheap grace" style of sacramental practice in the Catholic experience. He spoke and wrote of the increasingly dysfunctional approach to religious education in America: catechesis is often done without evangelization; children are the focus of such endeavors, without the involvement of their parents; and sacraments are celebrated without life change or conversion.

Reconciliation (or penance, or confession, as we once referred to it) is certainly one of the sacraments that frequently has been celebrated with cheap grace attitudes. Rarely did we reflect on the relationship between reconciliation and baptism, how reconciliation was recommitment to the original commitment of one's baptism. *Metanoia,* or turning from sin, in a real, existential sense, often was not part of the sacramental celebration. Attrition frequently outweighed contrition as the emotional, spiritual tone of the experience. Penitents often did not connect their sin with the larger context of the sin in the world or the need to transform the culture around them. Neither did we have much of an idea of how sacraments ought to ritualize and celebrate a person's growth into the church, the Body of Christ, the community of believers. Confession, like the other sacraments, was about "personal" salvation.

A Contemporary Understanding of Sin

Let us briefly return to the topics of sin and conscience formation. Many observers of the American Catholic scene portray contemporary American Catholics as increasingly selective in their attention to and appropriation of magisterial pronouncements. If this reading of the American scene is accurate (and I believe it is), I feel that there is both good and bad news in this development. The good news is that more and more Catholics are trusting the movement of the Spirit in their own lives. They are not letting pseudo-guilt and moral under-development prevent them from acting on the convictions of their own consciences.

The bad news is twofold. Some of these "selective Catholics" are not so much engaged in healthy conscience formation as they/we are swept up by the nonreflective whirlwind of consumerism and materialism. Not only are they/we selective about magisterial pronouncements, the deeper malaise is that they/we practice "smorgasbord discipleship" when it comes to the hard-core values of the gospel. I feel that parishes do not often provide forums in which people can come together to listen, talk, discuss, discern, and stretch morally. For example, because sexuality is a taboo subject when it comes to the religious education of our young people, because it is not an issue that is discussed openly and honestly and "up front," most Catholic youth are left to their own devices and resources to "patch together" some sort of working sexual morality. Recent studies, like Aaron Haas's *Teenage Sexuality* and Robert Coles and Geoffrey Stokes' *Sex and the American Teenager,* reveal an astonishingly high level of sexual activity among American teenagers. When asked to provide a rationale, moral conviction, or motivation for their behavior, many young people in both studies articulate a morality grounded in peer pressure and the values communicated by the mass media.

Humorists reflect on past days of Catholicism when there were "two great sins"—breaking the sixth commandment in any form and not fulfilling one's Sunday obligation. Our awareness of Scripture, psychology, and developmental theory have shown us how truly superficial our previous moral preoccupations were. The scriptural

view of sin reveals that sin is idolatry, hostility toward
one's fellow person, alienation and going it alone in life,
living illusion rather than truth, toxic competition, resent-
ment, jealousy; it is forgetting God, usually experienced on
both personal and communal-social levels. Parishes have a
responsibility to help disciples see, name, and turn from
those subtle, yet very real forces of evil in culture.
Engaging in discerning dialogue—with children, adoles-
cents, and adults—that attempts to add a critical, reflective
quality to our educational and ministerial efforts is an
absolute necessity for ministers who are serious about
helping others form conscience.

Moralist Father Timothy O'Connell in a recent article in
Chicago Studies distinguishes three different ways of understanding sin in the contemporary age. Sin is first of all,
he suggests, a *fact*. One need not be very wise or aged to
realize that evil is a *fact of life*. It is here in our world.
Daily living has led all of us to experience sin as a fact. *Sin
as fact* is close to what we have traditionally understood as
original sin. Sin is also an *act*. *Act* is to be understood in a
broad sense to refer to our personal involvement in the *fact*
of sin. Sin as act is our freely choosing to hold on to values
or engage in activities that are contradictory to how God
would have us be. Finally, sin, for O'Connell, can become
the very *direction* of a person's life. One's major
orientation in life can become *sinful*. Sin is a fact of life.
Sin is a personal *act*. Sin becomes the life *direction* of some
of us.

O'Connell still finds viability in the notions of *mortal
and venial sin*. He encourages contemporary Catholics to
interpret the notion of mortal sin according to exactly what
the word *mortal* suggests—*deadly*. In mortal sin, a kind of
death blow is dealt to one's integrity, to a relationship, or

to one's bond with God. If a deed or freely chosen value is not of such magnitude, it is to be considered venial.

Questions for Consciences

Conscience refers to one's inner processes of judging and deciding about moral right and wrong. Sometimes conscience operates proactively, that is, in anticipation of an upcoming decision or action. Sometimes conscience functions retroactively, remembering back to a past stance, action, or life pattern. I propose the following questions as guides for a kind of retroactive exercise of conscience, more commonly referred to as an examination of conscience.

1. What *attitudes, values,* or *life stances* within me could genuinely be considered self-centered, destructive, hurtful, or idolatrous?

2. What actions have I engaged in that has been self-centered, destructive, hurtful, or idolatrous?

3. Toward whom have these self-centered, destructive, hurtful, and idolatrous *attitudes and actions* been directed: myself? others? my relationship with God?

4. Have there been significant *single experiences* that stand out as sinful?

5. In what ways do I engage in *patterns* of sinfulness? What are recurring sinful patterns in my life?

6. What is *the level of moral seriousness* involved in what I discern as sinful in my life? Has my sin been seriously wrong, mortal sin; that is, has it seriously affected my self-definition and direction in life? Has it not been of that gravity?

7. What are my sins of omission: that is, what good have I missed doing? Do I conform to the wisdom of the world around me or challenge it and try to transform it?

8. What is the subtle sin that only God and I know about?

9. How do the hard sayings of Jesus make me feel, that is, his expectation that I play some small role in feeding the poor, clothing the naked, healing the sick, visiting the confined? Do I heed his warning not to invest my life in what ultimately does not matter?

10. Have I lived the essence of the moral vision of the Old and New Testament which call me to love of self, others, and God?

11. Do I act responsibly, or perhaps irresponsibly, with the gift of life?

12. Do I live the vision of life that Jesus called "the Kingdom"? Do I get lost in alternative visions of sexism, racism, militarism, consumerism, and materialism?

13. Do I consciously try to progressively deepen my conversion or turning toward God?

14. Do I live as a disciple, a person for whom Jesus makes a difference, a person appropriating and living the values of Jesus?

15. Do I live out the mission given me at my baptism to be salt, light, and leaven in the family, in the neighborhood, in the workplace? Am I committed to the Body of Christ, the Christian community?

Conscience—forming it or examining it—always involves keeping several things in tension: the moral vision of

Scripture (some of which is time-bound, like encouraging slavery and the oppression of women), the outer word or teaching authority of the church and its tradition, and one's inner word or convictions that flow from a person's unique gifts, experiences, personality, values, and religious experiences. Conscience is a process that involves this tension of several forces interacting with each other to result in moral decisions and behavior.

Discussion Questions

1. Jesus taught that it was hard for the rich to enter the Kingdom of God. In fact, a camel could more easily get through the eye of a needle. How can we reconcile this hard saying of Jesus with the materialistic, consumer-like lifestyles that most of us live?

2. This chapter stressed the subtle nature of sin. Discuss the subtle sin that is part of American life and institutions.

3. Name for yourself or your group the issues that you think ought to be confronted in an examination of conscience.

4. How do you discern the difference between mortal and venial sin?

Suggested Readings

Dietrich Bonhoeffer, *The Cost of Discipleship*
Robert Coles and Geoffrey Stokes, *Sex and the American Teenager*
Tad Guzie and John McIlhon, The Forgiveness of Sin
Aaron Haas, *Teenage Sexuality*
James Mackey, *Jesus: The Man and the Myth*
Karl Menninger, *Whatever Became of Sin?*
Timothy O'Connell, *Principles for a Catholic Morality*
M. Scott Peck, *People of the Lie*

Chapter Two

A HISTORY OF RECONCILIATION

Roots in Baptism

IN the early days of Christianity the ritual commonly understood to be related to the forgiveness of sins was baptism. A person was accepted by the community for baptism only after a discernible repentance from sin. Baptism ritualized, then, a changed life. The triple immersion in water of the early ritual spoke symbolically of a spiritual death to one way of life and a resurrection to a new way of life. Baptism spoke not only of the convert's repentance. It spoke also of God's love and forgiveness. The baptismal bath washed away the sin of the individual.

The Latin word *sacramentum* was used frequently in ancient Rome. It had two meanings for Romans. A *sacramentum* was, first of all, a pledge of money that the parties in a civil dispute would place in court custody (the winning party would win both sums). Second the term referred to a *vow* or *pledge* of allegiance that a Roman soldier took to the Roman emperor, to live and die for him and the empire. This latter connotation was appropriated by the early Christians during the first three centuries of the post-resurrection communities. *Sacramentum* came to be used to refer to the rituals that celebrated becoming a member of the Body of Christ. We know these rituals today as baptism, confirmation, and eucharist. It was the early Christian writer and thinker, Tertullian, who is recorded as first using the word *sacramentum* around the beginning of the third century. *Sacrament,* thus, replaced *mystery* as the common term for the rites of Christian initiation.

31

St. Paul's letters speak of baptism as a ritual of spiritual entrance into the life, death, and resurrection of Jesus. Paul believed the paschal mystery to be an ontological, salvific reality whose power was ongoing in the world and universe. Through baptism, a person shares in this salvific event. For Paul, baptism was likewise an immersion into the power of Jesus' Spirit. The baptized live a Trinitarian lifestyle, always "to the Father, through Jesus, in the Spirit." Baptism, for Paul, was incorporation into the church, conversion, the beginning of a new moral code and lifestyle, and the beginning of eternal life.

The use of water for rituals of sorrow and forgiveness did not begin with Christianity. The Old Testament Jews used a variety of water rituals to wash away sin and impurity. John the Baptist's baptism was a rite of preparation for the coming of the new age of the Messiah. Jesus in the Scriptures is portrayed as connecting baptism with taking on the identity of a disciple. St. Peter, in the second chapter of Acts, baptized approximately 3,000 people who had decided to convert and live this new way called Christianity. Evolving for about three centuries, the early Christian rites of initiation had more or less solidified form by the beginning of the third century. Thus from the Old Testament period, through John the Baptist, Jesus, to the early Christian era, water rituals were encouraged and used to "sign" turning from sin, forgiveness of sin, life change, and conversion.

The Era of the Catechumenate

The catechumenate, or Rite of Christian Initiation of Adults, which parishes have used since 1974 for the gradual formation of new members (converts), is a close approximation of the third-century style of preparation for and celebration of baptism. The third century is looked on now as the "golden age" of the catechumenate. Already in the fourth century the process and rituals of the catechumenate had begun to erode and disappear from popular experience. If there is any message to us in the ancient rites of initiation about how to understand sacramental practice it is that sacraments demand a *process*. More than holy things that people can receive without life change, sacraments are ritual, symbolic moments that both express conversion taking place and also nurture and foster the deepening of that conversion. Let us briefly consider the catechumenal process toward the sacraments of initiation, in the hope of discovering wisdom and implications for our experience of the sacrament of reconciliation.

In the early catechumenal communities a non-Christian was usually attracted to the new way of Christianity through informal association with believing, practicing Christians. In a gradual process of socializing, praying, worshiping, and studying the Word, nonbelievers gradually appropriated a kind of seminal, or basic faith in Jesus as Lord. This initial period, which ideally has no time limit put on it, is called in the 1974 revised rite, the period of *evangelization.* What was crucial in the first season of the journey toward baptismal initiation was the formation of loving relationships between those seeking membership in the Body of Christ and those who were already members. Also crucial was a basic *experience* of Jesus as truth for life. Community and religious experience, therefore, were the foundations for moving toward sacrament.

When this basic transformation, or primary conversion, was discerned by the community the seeker was accepted into a second stage or season of the journey. Rituals accompanied this transition, as they do now in the revised

Rite of Becoming Catechumens. In this second stage the Word and tradition were shared in more depth, and catechumens were invited to partake in the ministry of the community and its other activities. These first two stages or steps toward baptism often took up to three years.

A third stage of the process was and is a period of proximate preparation for initiation. The revised rite calls this period *illumination,* or *purification and enlightenment.* It consists of the Lenten season before the Easter vigil, when the sacraments of initiation are celebrated, as they were in the early church. This season, with its liturgies and mood of repentance, was and is a deepened experience of discipleship in which the catechumens, as well as the entire faith community, confront personal, communal, and societal sin, and seek to repent and turn away from idolatry in all of its obvious and subtle forms.

The rites of initiation in the early church consisted of integrated rituals that have come to be treated as separate sacraments. These rituals consisted of: immersion of the candidates in water, the laying of the bishop's hands on the heads of the newly baptized, anointing with chrism (now a distinct rite of confirmation), and first reception of eucharist. The immersion in water consisted of a triple plunging of the person in the baptismal waters, as he or she was baptized "in the name of the Father, and of the Son, and of the Holy Spirit." The person was held down in the water during each immersion to give the newly baptized an intense experience of baptism as death to old, sinful ways of living. The emergence from the water and putting on of a white garment spoke to all involved of how the ritual was an entrance into a new way of life. Finally the catechumenal process continue beyond Easter and the sacraments of initiation, called the *mystagogia* season in the new rite, a period of postbaptismal formation, continues until Pentecost. In this final period, neophytes are helped to find their place in the community of faith.

In addition to the importance of a process of conversion being joined to sacramental celebration, the ancient catechumenate and the revised rite teach us other things about the church's early approach to sacraments. Key to the catechumenal process is *discernment,* a prayerful watching, waiting, looking and listening, in community, about the quality, nature, and depth of one's conversion experience. Central also is the *integration* of ministries and ministers in a common mission of evangelization and conversion. Bishops, priests, deacons, religious, and community members engage in a number of evangelical, catechetical, liturgical, and pastoral-care ministries in an attempt to help each candidate find an environment where conversion might take place. The celebration of the sacrament in this process retrieves the ancient notion of sacrament as *vow.* Finally, in the journey toward initiation the *community* is intimately involved with the candidates. The community, present with the candidate at worship and at significant turning points in the journey with the candidates, becomes the true minister of conversion to the catechumens. During this journey, however, the catechumens, the sacramental pilgrims, become catalysts of reconversion for the community.

These important ingredients of sacramental theology and practice—conversion, discernment, multiple and integrated ministries, and community involvement—were lost as our sacramental system evolved. They are crucial, however, if we are to restore life and spirit to reconciliation and our other sacraments. We will return to these principles and the application of them to reconciliation in a later chapter.

The Decline of the Catechumenate
and Changing Sacramental Practices

By the fourth century the catechumenal process began to erode in different centers of Christianity. Several converging factors contributed to this erosion. The conversion of the Roman emperor Constantine in 312 and his Edict of Toleration more or less wedded the state and the church together. While this marriage perhaps provided the church with many new avenues for preaching the gospel, it also began to minimize the key catechumenal ingredients of discernment and conversion. In other words, genuine transformation of life, gradually developed under the influence of the Holy Spirit in interaction with and under the scrutiny of the community, ceased to be a high priority. The church lost some of its revolutionary, counter-cultural tonality, as, in effect, "everyone was becoming Christian." These early centuries of Christianity were also years marked by many heresies, or misinterpretations of doctrine. In an attempt to protect and pass on the pure Christian message, councils were convened and doctrines were articulated. The bishops and the gradually emerging priesthood, or presbyterate, increasingly became the defenders and teachers of the faith. This "clericalization" of teaching began to minimize the many diverse roles and ministries that were part of the catechumenal journey toward sacraments. In addition, conversion and the related movement toward the sacramental celebration of conversion became more of an experience of understanding doctrine than any sort of actual life change. The evangelization, illumination, and *mystagogia* became, in a sense, "excess baggage," unneeded pieces in an experience that became increasingly intellectual.

Tertullian and St. Augustine used the term "seal" to speak of one of the effects of baptism. Baptism brought with it a "seal." What was originally meant by the sacramental seal was somewhat similar to the seals, or marks of ownership, put on servants or military. As a soldier was, in effect, the property of the emperor and slaves were the property of their owners, so also Christians became Christ's for life, through baptism. As the church moved toward the medieval age, the word "character" was used to describe the lasting effect, not only of baptism, but also holy orders and matrimony. However, the notion of sacramental character is only one example of the metaphysical, ontological nature that the theology of sacraments took on. The original notion of "being sealed" by baptism had real, existential implications. One belonged to Christ. The issue of sacramental character became something rather far removed from the understanding or interest of ordinary people.

The Decline of Symbols

What also began with the decline of the catechumenate was a parallel decline in the power of the symbol. In Christianity and all religions, symbols help one to enter into mystery and experience the holy, God. In philosophizing about the effects of sacraments, the church weakened the power of the symbols used in ritual. The effects of ritual and symbols are, at least on a primary level, the experience that they bring to the people involved. The church, rather than allowing symbols to do what they can do naturally, began to define what effects the proper use of the symbols should produce.

The years 500 to 1,000 were a time in which the automatic effectivenes of the ritual was stressed. Pushed to an extreme, this sacramental style seemed almost magical in nature. It was this heavily philosophical, ecclesiastically legislated approach to religious experience and ritual which in the past gave birth to popular devotions among people. As sacraments became removed from the experience of people, simple peasants created their own rituals to express and nurture faith, commitment, and spirituality. It was this medieval style of sacramental life that also eventually gave rise to the protests of reformers like Luther, Zwingli, and Calvin.

The Council of Trent (1545–1563) was a reaction against the reformers. While it purified sacramental theology of some of its abuses and magical tendencies, it did not alter much "the holy thing that produces grace" mind-set of most people regarding sacraments. The thinking of St. Thomas Aquinas and other like-minded philosophers and theologians came to be known as "scholasticism." "Scholastic" vocabulary became the language with which sacraments were talked about. The reification of what used to be experienced as process was expressed in words like the "substance, accident, matter, and form" of sacraments. The current seven sacraments were not recognized as official Catholic sacraments, distinct from other rituals, until the second Council of Lyons in 1274. This teaching was reiterated at the Council of Florence in 1439 and the Council of Trent in 1547.

The Origins of the Sacrament of Reconciliation

As noted, Baptism was considered *the* sacrament of forgiveness in the early church. The kiss of peace and reception of communion were also looked on as sources of healing or forgiveness for minor flaws of conscience or moral behavior. Baptism and the process leading up to it were equivalent to a radical turning away from sin. In many instances St. Paul encourages his readers to "become new," "put on Christ," "die" to one way of life and rise to another. These are Paul's attempts to describe the once-for-all-time decision against sin that baptism represented. Baptism celebrated the convert's repentance, as well as his/her acceptance of God's forgiveness of sin. In 1 Corinthians 5 Paul goes so far as to advocate expulsion, or excommunication for a Christian who is "leading an immoral life, or is a usurer, or idolatrous, or a slanderer, or a drunkard." Paul goes on to say, "Of those . . . you can surely be . . . judges. . . . You must drive out this evil doer from among you" (vv. 11–13). A short time later, however, in writing 2 Corinthians, Paul advocates leniency in allowing an excommunicated member to return. "The punishment already is enough," Paul wrote. "The best thing now is to offer him your forgiveness and encouragement" (vv. 6–7).

Besides baptism as the main experience of repentance and forgiveness, the early church had other tools for reconciliation. The nation Israel, in living out the Old Testament law and moral code, developed many rituals and practices to facilitate moral conversion and reconciliation. As many other primitive religions did, Israel used purification rites, sacrifices, sin offerings, fasting, and almsgiving, among many other practices, as means of expressing and solidifying a turning from sin to God and covenant living. History also shows that in these Jewish communities rabbis held the power to "bind" and "loose." *Binding and loosing* referred to the rabbinic authority to include or exclude members from the community based on an individual's conformity with the community moral code. The early Christian community inherited Israel's rituals of purification and repentance, as well as the notion of *binding and loosing*. It should also be noted here that the practice of "confessing" sin was not an unknown phenomenon in Israel. The Jews had a Day of Atonement on which the priest of the community confessed his sins and the sins of the community, before offering sacrifice for those sins. Implicit in the Day of Atonement was a communal sense of *metanoia*, or desire to turn from sin to God. In addition, some Jews felt that individual confession of sin was a desirable practice. Leviticus 5:1–6 and Numbers 5:6–7 mention sins that ought to be confessed. In summary, repentance, acts of penance, excommunication, then reconciliation, and in some cases confession of sin, were values and practices of the communities in which Jesus grew up.

Inherited Customs and New Traditions

We really cannot speak of one uniform way that early Christian communities experienced reconciliation. There was diversity in the expression of this ministry. It is clear, however, that the early Christians inherited the penitential customs of the Israelite community and also inherited and adopted the notion of binding and loosing. Matthew 18:15 –18 is of importance in this analysis. Jesus said to the disciples: "If your brother should commit some wrong against you, go out and point out his fault, but keep it between the two of you. If he listens to you, you have won your brother over. If he does not listen, however, summon another, so that every case may stand on the word of two or three witnesses. If he ignores them, refer it to the

Church. If he ignores the Church then treat him as you would a gentile or a tax collector. I assure you, whatever you declare bound on earth shall be bound in heaven, and whatever you declare loosed on earth shall be loosed in heaven.''

In this short passage Matthew expresses a conviction that Jesus has bequeathed to the community a mission of reconciliation. Reconciliation is spoken of existentially and experientially. The responsibility for moral discernment, confrontation of each other's sins, discernment, and if need be, excommunication, belongs to the community. Fraternal correction is spoken of in progressive terms, beginning with individual dialogue and perhaps eventuating in expulsion from the community. Reconciliation, binding and loosing, seems to have been a personal and interpersonal responsibility and experience of the individual communities that formed in the name of Jesus.

But the second century carried with it distress that demanded new forms of reconciliation. Baptism was the experience of *first penance,* or turning from sin. The other penitential practices, brought over from the Jewish communities, complemented the primary conversion experience of baptism. In the second century the communities that we would now call the church had to face a new issue, that is, what to do with converts who had denied the faith to avoid persecution but wanted to return to active life in the Christian community. By the middle of the second century it had become rather common to readmit such people to the community after a lengthy process of ''reconversion'' that paralleled the catechumenate, the preparation for initiation into the church.

By the third century, a pattern for reconciling apostates

became somewhat set in the centers of Christianity. The
pattern of reconciliation, quite similar to the catechumenal
process of initiation, often included the following:

1) confession to a bishop

2) a process of life reform

3) exclusion from eucharistic sharing

4) the doing of penance, anywhere from several weeks
   to several years

5) discernment of when the candidate might be ready to
   return

6) imposition of hands by the bishop, symbolizing the
   readmission of the candidate to the eucharistic community and a new imparting of the Holy Spirit.

It should be noted that some of the penances given to sinners during this period were so harsh that they caused
people to abstain from the process or delay reconciliation
until their deathbed.

As the persecution of the church subsided with Constantine's acceptance of Christianity as the religion of the empire, the same rigorous process of reconciliation began to
be used for other sins: adultery, murder, idolatry, abor-
tion, and other sexual practices. Penances became quite
difficult for repentant sinners. There was divided opinion
in the various centers of Christianity as to whether such
sins could even be forgiven, or the sinner reconciled. Some
communities would not practice the reconciliation spoken
of here. Rather, sinners were thrown to the mercy of God.
For those communities that did engage in what is called

now "canonical penance," the actual penances were quite severe. In some communities, penances might include a forbidding of using public amusements, holding public office, or marital intercourse, or many years of fasting. In some communities bestiality carried with it, upon confession, at least thirty years of penance.

Again, there was an unevenness in the experience of reconciliation. These harsh penances were softened in some communities if the penitents could produce "letters from martyrs," or known witnesses to the faith, who pleaded for leniency for the sinner. In some communities stages of reconciliation were marked by identities sinners assumed for themselves. The experience of these stages lasted over years. In such communities an initial stage of repentance was to be a "weeper," someone who stood outside of the eucharistic gathering, unworthy to enter. A second stage was to become a "kneeler," one who knelt in repentance in the back of the assembly. A stage that was close to reconciliation with the community was the stage of "stander." In this stage a person could stay for a portion of the eucharist but had to highlight his sinful identity by standing.

Absolution or readmission to the community, was indeed a dramatic process and event in these centuries. In some communities it was granted by the bishop, only after discernment and election by the community. In addition, "second baptism or penance" was viewed as a once in a lifetime experience, certainly not something to be repeated. Because of the extreme penances, as well as the once in a lifetime nature of the experience, penitents were encouraged, and frequently chose, to not seek reconciliation with the church until close to death. Thus there were both fewer and fewer penitents and communicants, those who received the eucharist, in the church.

John Chrysostom, Irish Monks, and Soul Friends

St. John Chrysostom was one of the earliest proponents of repeated absolution, or readmission into the community. But the more weighty influence came from Ireland. Missionaries to the native Celts had begun a practice of soul-friending, or spiritual direction, as we would know it today. Included with the practice was private confession. Unlike earlier versions of reconciliation, such confessions were not "once in a lifetime" but could be repeated, based on the repetition of the sin. Private confession, while monastic in origin, did not need to be with a bishop or priest.

Thus, beginning in the sixth century, a Celtic-Irish practice began to spread to other parts of Europe. The penances connected with this style of reconciliation were frequently still quite difficult but not as long-term as in previous practices. This new-style, repeatable penance came to be known as tariff penance. Lists of customary tariff penances were gradually placed in manuals for more efficient implementation. These new penitential practices were not universally welcomed or accepted. The third Council of Toledo (a regional council) condemned repeated penances, and recommended the earlier practice of canonical penance. In the seventh century a synod at Calon sur Sauve in Southern France reacted similarly. In the same region a ninth-century council called for the reinstitution of public-canonical penance and condemned the use of the penitential manuals. Another council, in Paris, reiterated this condemnation. The controversy of once-for-all, public, canonical penance versus repeated, private penance raged for centuries in local churches and the universal church. In 1215 the Fourth Lateran Council officially endorsed private penance and required it once a year as part of the "Easter duty" of at least yearly reception of eucharist. The Council of Trent also formally affirmed the norm of private confession and absolution in 1551.

During this transition period regarding private confession, several subtransitions took place that should be noted. Between the years 1000 to 1200 (approximately) the words of forgiveness in this ritual were changed from "May God forgive . . ." to "I absolve you . . ." Priests increasingly took on the role of confessor in private penance, and their role changed from announcer of God's forgiveness to judge and more the medium of God's forgiveness. Some priests would refuse absolution on the grounds that true contrition was not present in the penitent. In a holdover from canonical penance, some sins were "reserved" and could be forgiven only by the bishop. The 1614 revised sacramentary taught that confessions were to be heard from behind a screen—to assure the anonymity of the penitent as well as to bridle the passions of confessors hearing the sins of penitent women.

The twelfth to the sixteenth centuries were times of theologizing—theorizing about the populist practices regarding penance. There was little doubt the pendulum had swung toward private, repeated penance. The theologian Abelard taught that it was contrition, not priestly absolution, that resulted in forgiveness of sin. Peter Lombard felt confession could be made to a lay person. While upholding the sacramental nature of private penance, he also felt forgiveness came through the penitent's contrition. Distinctions began to multiply in the church's teaching. Sin was distinguished by the terms *mortal* and *venial.* So also, contrition was divided between *perfect* and *imperfect* contrition. Punishment was spoken of as *temporal* and *eternal.* While priestly absolution removed the threat of eternal punishment, the justice of God still demanded compensation in the area of temporal punishment. This notion of temporal punishment fanned the small flames of the theology of purgatory, transforming it into a theological blaze in the church—an over-emphasized teaching for believers and a stumbling block for the reformers. A theology of indulgences flowed from the earlier church's practice of lessening penances through the letters of martyrs or Christian witnesses. Indulgences, like purgatory, led to theological distortions and abusive church practices.

Thomas Aquinas rose as a kind of synthesizer amid all this controversy. Aquinas taught that the sacrament of penance was constituted by both the confession of a person and the absolution of a priest. For forgiveness, contrition was needed on the part of the penitent. Even with absolution, however, people still suffered from a "hangover," or proneness to sin. While attrition was sufficient, in Aquinas' teaching, for the confession of sin, true contrition was necessary for forgiveness. Duns Scotus, another theologian, maintained that *attrition,* imperfect contrition, was sufficient for approaching the sacrament of penance. Then, through the sacrament, God provided grace *ex opere operato,* or through the ritual engaged in, which transformed the imperfect sorrow into true contrition. This latter opinion became the generally accepted theology and practice. Thus great emphasis developed around the absolution of the priest. Penance also became a sacrament that an individual "received" rather than actively engaged in as an expression of genuine conversion.

Summary of Major Trends and Shifts
from the Sixth to Sixteenth Centuries

With the expansion of tariff penance, beginning in the sixteenth century, penitential manuals were used by confessors. Specific penances were assigned to specific sins. The harshness and length of the penance was dependent on the degree of sin confessed. Therefore, in some cases, penances were every bit as long and severe as those administered during the period of canonical penance. But, since tariff penance dispensed with the practice of excluding the sinner from the community, the penances assigned more and more became disciplines for individual spiritual direction and interiorization. Penances that reminded the sinner of the social implications of sin became more and more rare. A major shift in the practice of penance was toward the repeatable nature of the experience. The once-for-all nature of penance ceased to exist. The bishop's role in the sacrament also was minimized. Penance became largely the responsibility of priests. Certain abuses grew up also in the doing of some penances. People would plead for shorter but more difficult penances to "get them done." Others would pay sums of money to compensate for the actual penance. Others would get servants to do the penance for them. The mind-set was a juridical one: all that mattered was the price for the sin being paid by someone.

During the early days of the tariff penance practice, absolution continued to be reserved until after penance was completed. There was great variation from one Christian center to another regarding the nature and length of penances for specific sins because of differences in the penitential manuals used. Some bishops had resisted tariff penance from the very beginning, advocating rather a return to canonical penance. The Council of Tours, in fact, in 813 called for a movement toward some uniformity in the penitential manuals. Other councils (Chalon, 813; Paris, 829) called for their banning. Finally, in the eleventh century, Pope Gregory VIII abolished their use.

But the abolishing of the penitentials shifted penance in a new direction. From the eleventh century on, while retaining some of the ingredients of both canonical and tariff penance, the ritual began to accelerate the imparting of absolution. Increasingly absolution was not delayed until penance was completed. The arduous and long penances were replaced by shorter ones, and often absolution was granted before the penance was begun. The individual priest confessor took on the role of *judge* as to the type of penance that was appropriate. The *process* that reconciliation or penance once was had taken even greater steps toward becoming "a holy thing" that people received. With these shifts, the "private penance" that many of us grew up with became the practice of the church. Thomas Aquinas, other scholastic thinkers, and other medieval theologians began to construct rather elaborate theologies around these evolving penitential practices.

The confirming of private penance as the church's normative style was significantly advanced in 1215 at the Fourth Lateran Council. The Council decreed that penance should be celebrated at least once a year, in tandem with the completion of one's eucharistic Easter duty. In 1439 a decree of the Council of Florence endorsed the Thomistic understanding of penance stressing: a) it is a sacrament, b) that demands contrition, c) confession to a priest, d) penance or satisfaction, and e) absolution by a priest. In the midst of this codification process, new problems arose concerning penance. The practices of *compen-*

sation and *substitution* relative to penance deteriorated into a misguided approach to indulgences applied to the temporal punishment due to sin. *Ex opere operato* thinking about absolution, that is, the conviction that the priest's absolution worked automatically in conveying God's forgiveness, was widespread. Absolution came to be stressed as more important than the sinner's repentance and conversion. People like Martin Luther and John Calvin, who witnessed these progressive distortions, were moved to speak out on the almost magical approach to sin and forgiveness into which the church was falling.

The Reformation and the
Catholic Counter Reformation

The medieval period was a time when Jesus' mandate to the community to "bind, loose, and reconcile," was re-translated into the "power of the keys." Jesus' giving to Peter "the keys of the Kingdom" came to be interpreted as a delegation of moral, juridical authority to the clergy of the church. This, as well as the abuses and distortions that had grown up, served to further alienate the soon-to-be reformers. This ecclesiastical attitude, as well as the prevailing scholastic theology, was rejected by Luther and others. Let us briefly examine the thinking of some of the reformers.

Luther

A) Luther seems to have maintained a generic sense of penance as a sacrament. As his approach to church developed, however, he came to recognize only two sacraments as initiated by Jesus: baptism and eucharist.

B) He also stressed that preoccupation with the role of the priest and the penitential works of the penitent de-

flected from the true experience of the sacrament, the
acceptance of the free gift of God's forgiveness.

C) Luther's theology emphasized the salvific effect of
Christ's life, death, and resurrection. The paschal
event paid the wages of sin. Penance was, for Luther,
more of a reminder to the penitent that through the
grace of God and the atoning death of Jesus he or she
was forgiven.

D) A key development in Luther's thought was his conviction that absolution, or the announcing of God's forgiveness, need not be reserved to ministers or priests
but was a power that ordinary Christians could exercise
with each other. All Christians had the power and right
to declare God's mercy to each other.

E) Luther continued to value the practice of confession
and absolution, according to his own adaptations. Lu-
therans, on the other hand, seem to have not seen the
value. The normative experience of forgiveness became
a general confession of sin at Sunday worship.

F) Luther began to minimize the importance of doing
penance as part of the sacrament, maintaining it was
an affront to the saving effects of Christ's death.

G) Luther rejected the Catholic notion of purgatory.

John Calvin

A) Calvin agreed with Luther that there was no scriptural
basis for a "Christ-instituted" understanding of penance.

B) The value of confession and absolution was in its
power to arouse feelings of faith and in its reminding
the sinner of God's grace and mercy.

C) Calvin maintained that general absolution at worship and individual absolution were of value, though absolution need not be administered by a priest.

D) He minimized the importance of confession according to species and number, advocating a more general confessing of sinfulness.

E) He repudiated the obligatory, yearly approach to confession, encouraging church members to see it more as a helpful option.

It should be noted that despite Luther's and Calvin's best efforts to salvage what they saw as valuable about the sacrament, their followers largely discontinued its use. The Anglican reformers adopted similar stands to those of Luther and Calvin, and by the eighteenth and nineteenth centuries it was largely ignored in this expression of Christianity also.

The Council of Trent (1545–1563)

The doctrine of penance with which many readers of this book grew up came from the Council of Trent's attempt to counter the theories, or what the bishops called the heresies, of the reformers. Pope Leo X named and condemned Luther's "heresies" in a papal bull, *Exsurge Domine,* in 1520. In the same year he excommunicated Luther. But it was not until 1551 that the Council of Trent synthesized official teaching in its *Doctrine on the Sacrament of Penance.* This document affirmed the following:

A) Christ instituted penance as a sacrament.

B) Contrition is required for confession.

C) Serious sins needed to be confessed according to species and number.

D) Satisfaction, or penance, is required for sin.

E) Only priests can administer absolution.

F) In a further attempt to endorse the role of the priesthood, the Council spoke of the encounter between
priest and penitent as juridical in nature. The priest indeed was a judge in a tribunal of justice. His activity in
the sacramental action operated *ex opere operato,*
somewhat automatically, as long as the penitent had
the proper interior disposition of repentance and contrition (*ex opere operantis*—referring to the attitude
and activity of the person "receiving" the sacrament).

Though the Tridentine version of the sacrament seems to
be a long way off from the penitential practices of the early
church, it should be noted that the medieval development
of penance did retain some ancient roots. These positive
values were retained in decrees that were obviously intended to discount and rebuke the Reformers' critiques:

A) Trent upheld and fostered an emphasis on contrition,
or sorrow for sin rooted in love.

B) The Council also propagated a conversion vision that
was oriented to the future. Penance was not to be just a
looking back, but also a projection forward. This
future orientation was especially articulated by the sinner's resolution to avoid the sins confessed in the
future.

C) Though "juridically packaged," the God image behind
Tridentine penance was a God of love and mercy, calling the sinner to a reciprocal love response.

However, Trent created both theological and practical problems in some of its statements:

1) The Council said the confession of serious sin to a priest was binding under *divine law.*
2) The confession of such sins according to number and kind was also spoken of as *divine law.*

Obviously, both scriptural and historical scholarship reveal such pronouncements to be time-bound and historically conditioned. They are more the defensive reactions of an institution being attacked than positive statements of theology and spirituality. History and tradition reveal that the church, from its inception, has had a variety of ways to experience repentance and penance and to celebrate reconciliation.

Chief among the Tridentine problems, however, was the legalization of the sacramental experience. The use of penitential manuals was replaced by a moralizing conscience formation and ecclesiastical forgiveness rooted in canon law. The church's sacramental life and moral life both became functions of canonical legislation. The confession according to number and kind, which enabled the "priest-judge" to determine an appropriate penance, resembled the rigidity present in the use of the penitential manuals.

The Tridentine style of penance often failed to convey the deeper dimensions of the sacramental encounter, namely forgiveness and healing. Also, in practice, penance and eucharist were often wedded in a distortion of the 1215 decree on the Easter duty. So, many Catholic faithful felt they were to receive communion once a year, and penance was to precede it. Even in the twentieth century, when some people began to receive communion more frequently, many felt confession had to precede communion. A movement started by a theologian, Cornelius Jansen, called Jansenism, influenced penitents' style of confessing and priests' style of absolving, even to our own day. Jansenism encouraged a greater scrupulosity about sin and greater rigorism about penance. This was particularly true in regard to sexual sin. Unfortunately, there is not much more history of penance to report from the Council of Trent until the time of the Second Vatican Council. The style of penance summarized in the preceding paragraphs more or less continued to be the church's practice until contemporary times.

Discussion Questions

1. What are your feelings and thoughts about the historical evolution of the sacrament? What periods raise positive feelings in you? Do any periods spark negative feelings?

2. Did reformers like Luther speak any truth about Catholic sacramental practice? If so, what?

3. Is there anything in the history of the sacrament of reconciliation that offers us direction or promise for the future of the sacrament?

Suggested Readings

Robert Duggan, *Conversion and the Catechumenate*
James Dunning, *New Wine, New Wineskins*
Leonce Hamelin, *Reconciliation in the Church*
Monika Hellwig, *Sign of Reconciliation and Conversion*
Richard McBrien, *Catholicism, Vol. II*
The Rite of Christian Initiation of Adults (United States Catholic Conference)

Chapter Three

VATICAN II AND BEYOND

VATICAN II's *Constitution on the Sacred Liturgy* (1963) articulated the Council's mandate for a revised rite of penance. *The Dogmatic Constitution on the Church* (1964) began to refocus the purpose of the sacrament, joining the traditional theme of *forgiveness* in the sacrament to *reconciliation* with God and the church. This early refocusing was a precursor of the revision of the rite, first published in 1973 and officially promulagted in the United States in 1976. The new Rite of Reconciliation was the last of the sacraments to be "renewed" by the work of the Council. The Council sessions extended from 1962 to 1965, but actual revisions took effect some eleven years after the Council formally concluded. *The Dogmatic Constitution on the Church (Lumen Gentium)*, is especially significant for our study in that it redefines the whole church as sacrament or sign and experience of God's presence, thus diminishing the "seven holy things" distortion of previous centuries. *The Constitution on the Sacred Liturgy* called for a renewal of all sacramental celebration so that the signs of the rituals might become more intelligible and meaningful for the people experiencing them.

The Rite of Penance

Before considering the new rite in detail let us consider some of the attitudinal shifts from the Tridentine format that are present in this rite. First, the role of the priest in the sacrament is considerably changed. The medieval version of the sacrament, which the church maintained into the current age, very much emphasized the priest as judge. The new rite presents the priest as healer, as a conduit of God's healing love and forgiveness. The focus of the sacrament is no longer sin, but experiencing and accepting *God's* love. The early church's emphasis on doing penance and the Tridentine emphasis on confession and absolution are held in balance with each other under the broader notion of reconciliation. Confession, absolution, and penance are among the many pieces or steps of the larger process of conversion from sin and reconciliation. The new rite reiterates Vatican II's emphasis on the *sacramentality* of the church. Reconciliation with God, therefore, is found through reconciliation with the church, the Body of Christ.

The Theology of the Rite of Reconciliation

The Congregation for Divine Worship prepared the *Rite of Penance*. The rite emphasizes the importance of repentance, conversion from sin, the doing of penance, and the experience of God's forgiveness in both the history of Christianity and the tradition of the Old Testament. For the Christian, Jesus is the person, the force through whom sinners can gain reconciliation with the Father. The church is the human locus where reconciliation with the Father, through Jesus, can now be experienced. The rite speaks of baptism as the primordial experience of forgiveness of sin. Quoting St. Ambrose, the authors say that the waters of baptism and the tears of penance both lead to forgiveness and reconciliation. The church is both holy and sinful—in constant need of purification.

The church has at its disposal many means to accomplish ongoing repentance and reconciliation: personal struggles endured with faith, acts of penance, prayer, use

of Scripture, and the church's liturgical and sacramental
life. The notion of human and supernatural "solidarity" is
spoken of in the introduction to the rite. The human family has a solidarity in sin. This solidarity in sin results in the
human family and members of the church harming each
other and the general well-being in attitudes and behaviors
opposed to God's Kingdom. But Christians also have a solidarity in repentance and reconciliation. The church is, in
fact, a sign of conversion and reconciliation to the world.

The new theology of reconciliation reiterates the traditional components for the complete celebration of the sacrament: 1) contrition (heart-felt sorrow and *metanoia*);
2) confession, following inner examination; 3) acts of penance or satisfaction that are joined to changed behavior
and an attempt at repairing harm caused to others by sin;
4) absolution, a tangible sign, given through a minister, in
which God's forgiveness is shared with the repentant
sinner.

Those who can benefit from the sacrament are both
those who have severed their bond with God through serious sin, or those who wish to more sincerely seek holiness
and turn from less serious sin. Paragraph seven of section
II of the rite's introduction states: "The faithful must confess to a *priest* each and every grave sin which they remem-
ber. . . . This sacrament is also very useful as a remedy for
venial sins." Thus the centrality of the role of the priest is
maintained in the revised rite. However, the rite does speak
of the whole community of faith partaking in a larger,
more generalized ministry of reconciliation. The ministry
of the sacrament of penance belongs to bishops and priests
acting in communion with their bishops. Priests must have
the faculty to absolve, in accordance with canon law; that
is, they must have official delegation from the local

bishop. In danger of death, bishops and priests can absolve any place, at any time. The rite encourages confessors to prepare well to share in Christ's ministry of reconciliation, realizing the priest is in the position of guide and shepherd on peoples' moral journey and search. Prayer, as well as other preparation, should be engaged in so that the confessor can really help a person in the process of moral discernment. While the role of healer is emphasized for the priest, the role of *judge* is not completely eradicated in the new rite and is spoken of several times in the document.

The revisions of the seventies necessitated some physical reconstruction in many churches. While retaining the option for "behind the screen" confessions in confessionals, many communities, to enrich the mood and environment for "face to face" experiences of the sacrament, have prepared "reconciliation rooms." While the quality of these rooms varies from place to place, most are so designed to enhance the positive nature of the sacrament, rather than the darkness and fear associated with the confessional. In discussing the *time* for celebrating reconciliation, the document discourages the practice of having reconciliation being conducted simultaneously with the eucharist. The Lenten season is stressed as a particularly good time to underscore the value of the sacrament for the faithful. This Lenten emphasis does not spring from concern for "the Easter duty," but rather an appreciation of the liturgical year and the tone of conversion and repentance present in the Lenten season.

Four Styles of Celebrating Reconciliation

Some liturgists have indicated that during the preparation of the rite there was strong opinion on the part of some of the consultants that the revisions provide two formats for reconciliation: general confession and absolution as the norm, and individual confession and absolution for those with serious moral struggles or those in spiritual direction. The final version of the revisions, however, offers four formats. The four formats have failed to spark much new enthusiasm for the reconciliation process, however.

A. *Rite for the Reconciliation of Individual Penitents*

This "one on one" experience of the sacrament can be in the traditional confessional or in a reconciliation room. After adequate preparation on the part of both priest and penitent, the ritual proceeds according to the following steps:

1. *Welcoming of the Penitent.* These few moments of mutual greeting often are informal in nature, unlike the formal, ritualistic "Bless me, Father . . ." of by-gone years. Older or more traditional people should be allowed to retain such a format as part of the revised ritual if they are more comfortable with such a practice.

2. *Sharing the Word of God.* This is perhaps the most dramatic and welcome addition to celebrating reconciliation. Adaptation is encouraged relative to this component. Scripture may be read by the penitent during *preparation* for the sacrament or during the *actual celebration*. The priest may be the one to proclaim the Scripture during the ritual. The choice of texts may be by priest or penitent. Whatever the scriptural text (and some are suggested in most editions of the rite), its purpose is to reenforce the stance of contrition and repentance as well as the awareness of God's unconditional love and forgiveness.

3. *Confession of Sin and Penance.* The rite encourages penitents to make a complete confession, obviously men-

tioning all serious sins. The priest can share words of guidance, if that seems needed or appropriate. He then suggests a penance. The rite offers the following guideline for penances: a) they should be such as to include satisfaction for sin (making up for sin, in a sense of justice) and also have a therapeutic effect (that is, to reorient the person away from sin); b) prayer and/or self-denial, and/or works of mercy are suggested as viable means of penance; c) works of mercy are, in fact, encouraged to remind the penitent of the social nature of sin; d) the penance in some way should correspond to the gravity of the sin.

4. *Prayer of the Penitent and Absolution.* The penitent verbalizes contrition and sorrow in prayer. This prayer can be a memorized formula, be spoken spontaneously, or be from Scripture—for example a psalm.

The suggested words of absolution are: "God, the Father of mercies, through the death and resurrection of his Son has reconciled the world to himself and sent the Holy Spirit among us for the forgiveness of sins; through the ministry of the church, may God give you pardon and peace; and I absolve you from your sins in the name of the Father, and of the Son, and of the Holy Spirit." The penitent responds "Amen."

The new words of absolution reflect the hybrid theology and practice suggested by the revised rite. The traditional, "May our Lord Jesus Christ absolve you, and by his authority I absolve you from your sins," stressed the transcendence of God and the authority of the confessor coming from God. The newer words stress the mercy of God, as well as the salvific effect of the life, death, and resurrection of Jesus. Absolution is presented as part of a bigger process—reconciliation. The Holy Spirit is spoken of as the agent of conversion, and the power through which forgiveness is extended to the sinner. Finally, "the ministry of the church" is the vehicle of God's grace and forgiveness. The ministry of reconciliation is the activity, the responsibility of the whole church. Some of the words of absolution, however, reflect a clinging to the juridical, clerical emphasis on absolution. Reconciliation is at once the work of the church, but, in a special way, the job of the priest. The rite strikes a balance between retrieving past richer notions of reconciliation, while also maintaining some of the trappings of the medieval style. The priest's words of absolution are both an extension of God's healing love and a juridical declaration of release from the pain and punishment due to sin.

It should be noted that provision is also made for the use of the "essential" words of absolution if circumstances dictate brevity. They are: "I absolve you from your sins in the name of the Father, and of the Son, and of the Holy Spirit. These essential words can be used whether the long form of the rite or a shorter form, in the case of necessity, is being used. In an attempt to emphasize the healing nature of this encounter, the priest extends either both hands or his right hand over the head of the penitent during the words of absolution. Many clergy actually lay hands on the penitent, sharing with him or her "the embrace of God."

5. *Proclamation of Praise and Dismissal.* Forgiveness is a gift from God. The rite especially highlights this in its encouragement to the penitent to offer praise and thanks to God after absolution for the gift of forgiveness. Again, this may follow a formula provided in a prayer book or other resource, or be spontaneous. As in other sacraments, an obvious dismissal is encouraged in which the celebrant sends the person into the world, to his or her relationships, and into life, to live a better life, more in conformity with the gospel.

B. *Rite for Reconciliation of Several Penitents with Individual Confession and Absolution.*

This second form of the rite can be used for groups of people who experience most of the components of the sacrament together but confess their sins and accept absolution individually. The same phases of the sacramental experience used in the first format are present also in this version. The communal context is the significant change. Here also we see the designers of the rite striking a compromise or producing a theological-sacramental hybrid. The communal setting is a powerful reminder of the social and ecclesial nature of sin, that we do not sin in a vacuum. The insistence on individual confession and absolution reasserts the Tridentine vision and style.

The communal format provides opportunities that the individual rite does not. Because of the liturgical context of the experience, music is often added, which can profoundly influence the imaginations and spirits of those gathered. A homily can be added to bring the Scripture that is proclaimed into better focus and to re-echo the call to repentance and the good news of God's love. Following the homily, time is given for examination of conscience. This examination can be done in silence, or the celebrant or other minister can provide some guidance or suggestions for moral discernment and reflection. Whatever form of the rite is used, it is important to suggest that the examination of conscience be anchored in and refer to Scripture. In this second format, the examination is followed by a common prayer of sorrow—either the "I confess . . ." prayer, or some other, and the Lord's prayer.

Individual confession, absolution, and assigning of penance follow this shared prayer. Usually other confessors are present at such services to facilitate the numbers of people who may want to confess. When all confessions are completed, the celebrant returns to the sanctuary to lead the congregation in prayers of praise and thanksgiving. Subsequent to these prayers, he dismisses the congregation.

While these celebrations seem to be popular with those who value the sacrament, experience with this format has shown some practical difficulties. Long lines of penitents at such services have robbed the rituals of some of their potential for religious experience. The bringing in of outside confessors lends an impersonal tone to a ritual that is supposedly focused on the communal, relational nature of sin. The frequent antidote of suggesting to people that they "just mention one sin," without even sitting down to talk to the priest resembles more a moral car wash than a celebration of the Lord's forgiveness. Despite frequent reminders to not use these sacramental moments to seek personal counsel, many people still do. This antagonizes people still waiting for confession and creates tension for the confessor, who is both trying to be sensitive to the individual while also being sensitive to the feelings of the congregation. Finally, frequently the closing prayers of praise and the dismissal are not experienced by many people who fail to wait for the closing of the service. Some of these practical difficulties are lessened by a more frequent offering of such services and by not waiting for the week before Christmas and Easter to hold communal reconciliation.

C. *Rite for Reconciliation with General Confession and Absolution*

The rite states clearly that the ordinary way to celebrate reconciliation is through individual, integral confession and absolution. The rite does make provision for general confession and absolution in particular circumstances: the danger of death, or the penitents so out-numbering the confessors that a fitting sacramental celebration is impossible. Mission areas are especially indicated as places where this format might be used. The ritual notes that large numbers should not be used as a frequent excuse for general absolution. Large numbers serve as a rationale only when the situation would make a fitting celebration impossible and therefore deprive people of a needed use of the sacrament. Each bishop can decide on the particular interpretation of and implementation of these guidelines. The use of general absolution for any other reasons must be negotiated through the ordinary or his delegate (vicar, dean, etc.). In the case of serious sin, a penitent must individually confess such sins within a year. General confession and absolution contain all of the elements in the previous two versions of the rite. The *Confiteor,* or its equivalent, can be used as a general confession. Penitents are asked to show some sign of wanting and accepting absolution, i.e., kneeling, bowing, etc.

While church officials seem to minimize the value and pastoral effectiveness of this version, it has been my experience that such celebrations can be quite powerful. I say this with deep personal regard for and valuing of the individual rite. There seems to be a kind of implicit mistrust of Catholic people's celebration of this rite on the part of liturgists and hierarchy. I have found that, rather than trying to "get off easy" with general absolution, those with serious moral problems actually seek out the counsel of one of the confessors after the service, or at a later time. It is certainly also a quite appropriate celebration for those who do not have serious sin to confess. Over and over again, people have made comments to this effect: "I feel more forgiven after this service than I would having waited in line to talk individually to the priest." I personally believe that general confession and absolution ought to be pastorally used with

greater frequency. Perhaps the growing clergy shortage
will transform many more areas of the country into "mission areas" and, in effect, necessitate the more frequent
use of this version of the rite.

D. *Nonsacramental Penitential Celebrations*

This fourth form of liturgically celebrating reconciliation
does not involve absolution. It is, in essence, a celebration
of the Word with an emphasis on encouraging people to repent and accept God's forgiveness in their lives. Such penitential services can be used to foster a spirit of penance,
prepare for a later confession, and aid in conscience formation with children, adults, and catechumens.

While there is great advantage in these services, religious
educators have great difficulty distinguishing them from
sacramental services in explaining them to adults and children. The rather narrow understanding of sacrament, intimately tied to the priest's absolution, is a curious notion
for many of the faithful. The filter through which so many
contemporary people experience life is an existential-phe-
nomenological one. If a penitential service like the one we
are discussing helps a person to feel God's love and begin
to turn from a particular type of sinfulness, I think it can
be truly a sacramental encounter for that person. I am
speaking here of sacrament in a broad incarnational sense,
an event in which mystery is mediated.

The introduction to the rite concludes with some practical considerations. Episcopal conferences are to collabo-
rate in the establishment of regional norms and regula-
tions. Bishops are charged with setting standards for the
diocese in keeping with expectations of the episcopal conferences. Again, special mention is given in this section
regarding the cautious use of general absolution. It is the
responsibility of priests to adapt the rite and use it wisely in

specific pastoral settings, as well as to provide opportunities for parish celebrations of the sacrament. Here also priests are reminded of the extraordinary circumstances needed to justify the use of general absolution and the necessity of reporting having used it to the bishop or his delegate.

1983 - The Sixth General Assembly
Synod of Bishops

The synod of bishops of 1983 was held in a year marked as a special Jubilee Year celebrating redemption. Consultation with episcopal conferences and synods around the world revealed much pastoral and episcopal concern over the infrequent use of the sacrament worldwide and also a diminishing sense of penance. Because the Jubilee Year and the synod coincided in time, the connection between redemption and reconciliation was discussed a great deal by church leaders. In preparation for the synod, in January of 1983 Pope John Paul II sent to all who would attend the synod a document officially known as an *Instrumentum Laboris*. An *Instrumentum Laboris* is a synthesis of Catholic thinking on a given topic developed after consultation with local churches, leaders, and theologians around the world. The letter summarized the thinking of the local churches, the bishops, and the Roman Curia on the subjects of reconciliation and penance.

The document was entitled *Reconciliation and Penance in the Mission of the Church*. It was made available to the bishops who would attend the synod, all other bishops, the local churches, and the faithful at large. This 1983 document was divided into three sections:

1) The World and Humanity in Search of Reconciliation

2) The Announcement of Reconciliation and Penance

3) The Church, Sacrament of Reconciliation

We will briefly consider each of the subsections.

The World and Humanity in Search of Reconciliation

This part of the *Instrumentum Laboris* analyzes the divisive world that we live in. Societies, cultures, nations, and families display an alarming estrangement or alienation from each other. Tensions and divisions abound in our world. Even among the various denominations of Christianity there are conflicts. The contemporary tendency is to explain away the violence, hurt, and injustice that such alienation causes. We can rationalize by saying all evil is systemic and that people turn to sin in an attempt to protect themselves from the sin of systems and organizations. Sinners, in a sense, adopt the wisdom of the world for survival. Another typical pattern is to psychologize sin away or minimize the reality of evil by finding its roots in psychological disorders that our out of our control. The world needs to discover again that the root cause of much of the world's maladies is sin. Sin is an objective fact of our lives. Sin is also profoundly personal. While we may be the victims of sin on occasion, we also personally victimize others through sin. Rather than passively accepting sin as a fact over which we have no control, or denying the reality of sin, we need to take responsibility for our own actions, specifically our sin.

Sin holds the human person in bondage, away from the self he or she is meant to become and away from God the source of good. The only fitting antidote to sin and its worldwide consequences is reconciliation with God. In turning from sin to God, through conversion and penance, people begin to both discover their own integrity and restore the world order to peace, justice, and integrity. Essential to the mission of the church is to serve as an instrument of this reconciliation to those who are members of the church and to the entire world.

The Announcement of Reconciliation and Penance

In 2 Corinthans 5:18–20, Paul wrote: "God . . . through Christ has reconciled us to himself and gave us the ministry of reconciliation; that is, God was in Christ reconciling the world to himself, not counting their trespasses against them, and entrusting to us the message of reconciliation. . . . We beseech you on behalf of Christ, be reconciled to God." By mandate from Christ, the church announces the good news of the forgiveness of sins. Reconciliation with God and reconciliation of human beings with each other has been realized in the death of Jesus. Through baptism, we spiritually share in this accomplishment. But human nature is such that the baptized fall back into sin. The church's mission to the world is to both announce what Christ has done for us and remind a sinful church that the only way to continue in life as a "new creation" is an ongoing discipline of conversion and penance. God has taken the initiative through Jesus in extending reconciliation to the world. The call of the church to the sinner is to be responsible for one's own moral integrity and spiritual discipline. The ministry of the church seeks to help the human family rediscover the moral imperatives and norms that are deep within every heart, though often not attended to. Reconciliation is both personal and social. It is individuals seriously engaged in their own work of reconciliation that will begin to share the fruits of redemption with society and transform the world.

This section of the document closes with a rather strong

statement that the sacrament of reconciliation is an obligation mandated by Christ and part of the order of salvation
intended by the Father. Again, while upholding the value
of the sacrament, I feel that such a statement would have
to be looked on as a theological interpretation rather than
as historically accurate.

The Church: Sacrament of Reconciliation

In this third, and perhaps most helpful, subsection the
document speaks much more practically and existentially
of the church's "ministry of reconciliation." The church
is, in essence, Christ's sacrament, sign and instrument of
reconciliation in the world. The church exercises this
ministry in three ways:

1) by announcing salvation in a prophetic way;
2) by celebrating penance in a variety of ways, but especially through the sacraments; and
3) by witnessing to a reconciled life and promoting reconciliation in the various spheres of social and personal life.

We will consider each of these functions briefly.

1. The Prophetic Message of Reconciliation

The church's proclaiming the Word of God, the good
news that reconciliation is possible through Jesus, that
penance and conversion are the posture of the true disciple, is itself a reconciling act. This prophetic ministry is
counter-cultural in its invitation to both individuals and
societies to appropriate the reconciled state offered as gift
through Jesus.

2. *Penance in the Sacraments and the Life of the Church*

In a retrieval of our roots as church, the document speaks of baptism as our foundational sacrament of reconciliation. Christ's victory over sin is first experienced sacramentally in baptism. Baptism is a ritual of beginning. It begins a life that very consciously pursues sanctity, holiness, and Kingdom living. Secondary reconciliation can be experienced through the sacrament of reconciliation. Re-echoing the tradition of the early Christian community, the *Instrumentum* speaks of the sacrament as a healing, therapeutic experience for us who sin even after baptism. The eucharist is also spoken of in this section. In its re-presenting and memorializing of the Good Friday to Easter passage of Jesus, the eucharist is a profoundly reconciling experience—offering to those who partake a share in the salvific Christ event.

Besides sacraments, however, there are other practices and traditions in the daily life of the church which are or can be reconciling moments. There are nonliturgical experiences of making peace with God and others. The document lists the penitential seasons of Advent and Lent, prayer, fasting, almsgiving, meeting the needs of others, paying the price of engaging in works of justice, and carrying the cross of daily struggles in our personal, relational, and professional lives all as opportunities for reconciliation. It also points out, however, that many of these practices have fallen into disuse in contemporary Catholicism.

This section includes a polemical piece on the value of individual confession. While this emphasis seems to me overstated in the recent official documents on reconciliation, this section speaks of a value in individual confession that I have also found to be psychologically and spiritually healthy—that is, the value of the verbal expression of ones inner life, in this case, specifically sin and sorrow. In another book, *Spirituality for an Anxious Age—Into Your Hands,* I write of the importance of listening to our own inner workings and naming and sharing them with others as a way of avoiding the anxiety and stress that comes from repressing and suppressing our inner selves. Therapists regularly aid clients in *ventilation* and *cartharsis*—the release of pent-up thoughts and feelings. In psychotherapy and counseling clients report that the verbal expression that is part of ventilation and catharsis is in itself a source of relief and healing. The A.A. program and other support groups that model themselves on A.A. have as one of their therapeutic steps the careful inventory of one's moral life and the sharing of one's flaws and vices with one trusted other. Perhaps this might serve as a folksy principle that supports the value of individual confession: what we are unwilling to share with at least one other trusted person, we probably are trying to avoid or not pay attention to ourselves.

This section on penance in the life of the church and in sacramental celebration concludes with a reiteration of the revised rite's caution concerning general absolution. There are also statements on both the value of devotional confessions for venial sin and catechesis for the experience of sacramental reconciliation for young children as they reach the age of reason and prepare for first eucharist. An unfortunate conclusion or interpretation that could flow from the theology of this piece is due to the misconception that reconciliation must always precede eucharist. A parochial high-school teacher in the inner city of Chicago told me that this medieval misconception was both the conviction and sacramental practice of many Hispanic young people and their parents.

3. *Witness of a Reconciled Life and Promoting Reconciliation in the Spheres of Personal and Social Life*

The most important ministry we can do is often far from the church buildings. It is in the marketplace. Disciples are indeed not a group of elite privatists. We are "for the world." Personal conversion is incomplete without a dedication also to transforming society. The converting, reconciling person is in the process of becoming a new creation who lives under the sway and influence of God's grace. In this evolving process a person takes on the identity of a witness to the Kingdom. A reconciled life is a sign to the world.

Christians need, however, to not only witness but also to actively promote reconciliation. Some concerns in this area of promoting reconciliation are these: improving catechesis on the many dimensions of reconciliation—as activity of the church and sacrament; fostering a renewed spirit of reconciliation and penance; and focusing peoples' attention on various spheres of life that cry out for reconciliation. These include personal living; family life; social life, those areas concerned with social justice; parish; groups and associations; dioceses; religious communities; ecumenism, the church's relationship with Protestant churches and non-Christian groups; and the church's relationship with the nations of the world in our common effort toward peace.

Conclusion

In an address given on August 10, 1983 on the topics of the document just discussed and the approaching synod, Cardinal Joseph Bernardin of Chicago emphasized the importance of a key theme in the *Instrumentum Laboris,* that is, the *sacramentality of the church.* Cardinal Bernardin stated that unless people begin to understand the church as sacrament, the mediator of forgiveness and grace, they will never understand or appreciate the sacrament of reconciliation. The sacrament can only be understood and appreciated within the broader context of the church. The church is healer; guide; proclaimer of the message of forgiveness; reparation for a world flawed by sin; discerner and judge of the signs of authentic conversion. The liturgical sacramental moment must be seen against this broader context, as well as the longer process that we call conversion.

1984 - Apostolic Exhortation on Reconciliation and Penance by John Paul II

John Paul II's apostolic exhortation reiterates much of the thought of the *Instrumentum.* I would like, however, to share some of his special points of emphasis. The Pope, like the authors of the synodal document, begins with an analysis of the shattered world in need of reconciliation. He names the root cause of the divisions among people and throughout the world. It is only individuals confronting personal and social sin, and turning from sin, that will eventually lead to a reconciled world.

John Paul tries to pin down a somewhat precise understanding of certain terms. Penance is an ascetical expression of conversion. After the insights and the decision that lead to conversion have been arrived at, a person must *do* something to change not only heart but also lifestyle. *Reconciliation* is a renewed state of oneness with one's self, others, and God. *Conversion* and *penance* lead to this situation or experience of *reconciliation.* The three terms refer to stages or periods in a process, which is a breaking from sin and turning toward God and love.

Included in the exhortation is a pastoral reflection on the

Prodigal Son parable from the gospel of Luke. The father who seeks out the returning prodigal son obviously is a reflection of the way the God of Jesus is: He loves the selfish, ungrateful son with a nonmeasuring, gratuitous love that seems almost inappropriate after the youngest son's narcissistic breaking away from the community. It is obvious that the prodigal son is a reflection of us—the sinful disciples, who willfully break bonds with both the Father (God) and the family (the community). It is perhaps less obvious, but emphasized by the Pope, that the jealous elder son also reflects us. The human standards for strict justice that we attempt to put on God simply do not fit. Though the younger son deserved a more just response from the Father, justice was tempered by unconditional love. The just, and also proud, elder son could not understand the father's (God's) unconditional love. His inability to understand his father was probably also a reflection of his own subtle sin. Though obviously responsible and dedicated (religious), he could not let go of hurts and resentments to welcome his brother in love. His self-righteousness is equally as divisive as the younger son's self-centeredness.

The theme of the church as the "sacrament of reconciliation" is reiterated. Reconciliation is the mission of the church. The church is the sign and means of reconciliation. The church acts as sign and means of reconciliation by a) living as reconciled communities, thus giving witness to the world; b) by engaging in service to the world and proclaiming the good news of salvation and reconciliation; c) by administering the seven sacraments; and d) by prayer, spiritual discipline, and concern for and involvement in peace and justice. The church proclaims to the world, in a variety of ways, that God's love is greater than sin.

Using Old Testament stories of sin, John Paul explains sin as, in essence, a turning from God—no matter how subtle or disguised that turning might be. His theologizing reminds one of the thinking of the Protestant theologian, Paul Tillich, who described sin as idolatry, or giving someone or something the *ultimate concern* that should be given only to God. This rupture with God can only lead to rupture with other people and also with one's best self. The Pope classifies sin as *personal* and *social* (often found in societal systems and institutions), and *mortal* and *venial.* Though he accepts a more current understanding of mortal sin as severing one's bond with God, he cautions against simply equating mortal sin with a seriously sinful life option, or choice of life direction. In addition to fundamental option, people can commit mortal sin by willingly choosing something "gravely disordered" which implicitly carries within itself a rejection of God and his law. The loss of the sense of sin in our world is due to a number of secularist forces. Perhaps one of these forces, the Pope suggests, is the modern church's minimizing of the reality and potential for mortal sin.

In the *mysterium pietatis* (the mystery of our religion), a notion from Paul's first *Letter to Timothy,* God has taken the reconciling initiative toward us in the redemptive incarnation, death, and resurrection of Jesus. Our part of the *mysterium pietatis* is to respond with dispositions and behavior that lead to a reconciled life.

It is through dialogue on all levels of church life, proper catechesis, all the sacraments—but especially the sacrament of reconciliation—that the church can foster the spirit and practice of reconciliation. John Paul states clearly in section III, paragraph 30 that Jesus has given us the sacrament of forgiveness. In paragraph 31, he expresses a conviction that for the Christian, the sacrament of reconciliation is the ordinary means of reconciliation after serious sin. He reiterates that *contrition* is the key value needed from the penitent and that the proper disposition of the priest is that of both *judge* and *healer*.

Finally, in paragraph 32, he speaks to the issue of the forms of the sacrament. He speaks of the individual form as the ordinary, normal way of celebrating the sacrament —never to fall into disuse. The second form, communal celebration with individual confession and absolution, is spoken of as really the equivalent of form one, with communal aspects added to highlight the communal nature of both sin and reconciliation. Form three, or general confession and absolution is exceptional in nature, the Pope says, not to be arbitrarily used, but only in conformity with special discipline.

We have charted the historical evolution of the sacrament of reconciliation as well as its revision as a consequence of Vatican II; we have also looked at the latest magisterial pronouncements on the topic. We move next to a consideration of the way reconciliation is being experienced now in both parishes and the marketplace. We will look also at issues and hard questions related to reconciliation that we must confront as we approach the future.

Discussion Questions

1. Reflect on or discuss the four options for celebrating reconciliation provided for in the 1976 revised rite. Did the revisions go too far? Did they go far enough?

2. What are your thoughts and feelings on general absolution?

3. The 1983 bishops' statement speaks of the need the world has for reconciliation. Discuss.

4. John Paul II presents the self-righteousness of the elder son as destructive as the selfishness of the prodigal son. A true spirit of penance and reconciliation demands a healthy humility. What is humility?

Suggested Readings

Pope John Paul II, *Apostolic Exhortation on Reconciliation and Penance*

Constitution on Sacred Liturgy (United States Catholic Conference)

Dogmatic Constitution on the Church (United States Catholic Conference)

Rite of Penance (United States Catholic Conference)

Chapter Four

RECONCILIATION IN THE CONTEMPORARY CHURCH AND IN THE FUTURE

Now and the Future

THE University of Notre Dame's Institute for Pastoral and Social Ministry and Center for the Study of Contemporary Society have been engaged in a study of American parish life that began in 1981 and will continue until 1988. Some of the research results, which have begun to be released, are quite interesting.

1) Unpaid lay people conduct many of the important ministries in a contemporary parish.

2) While responsibility for ministry is being shared, policy control still lies largely in the hands of the clergy.

3) Parish boundaries still influence the lives of most Catholics, though some choose to worship in neighboring churches on occasion for a variety of reasons.

4) Twenty-four percent of the people surveyed in this 1,100 parish sample are involved in spiritual renewal programs, prayer groups, or Bible study.

5) Over 85 percent felt that the parishes that they belonged to filled their spiritual needs, but 46 percent said the parish failed to meet their social needs.

6) Though there are differences of opinion as to what ministries should be done by whom, there is little anger or uneasiness about liturgical change now.

7) There is evidence that at least in small numbers Catholics are awakening to social issues and questions of peace and justice.

8) Close to 50 percent said that they wished the parish had more skilled staff people on hand who could engage in ministries of individual and family guidance and healing.

The openness to both lay ministry and liturgical innovation, plus the expressed hunger for healing and guidance are important issues for the parish to consider in its responsibility to continue the mission of reconciliation entrusted to us by Jesus. Reconciliation is about much more than a sacrament. It is the fruit of many of the church's ministries and needs to be done in a variety of ways, based on the local community's needs and wounds.

Participation in Religious Rites in the Contemporary Church

The Notre Dame study relies on the General Social Surveys (GSS) of the National Opinion Research Center at the University of Chicago for data on the general Catholic population's participation at Mass and other liturgical functions. The GSS is held in high esteem by most social scientists.

Attendance at Eucharist

The 1982–84 GSS showed that 27 percent of adult Catholics and 30 percent of adult Protestants attend church services once a year or never. Forty-four percent of adult Catholics and 37 percent of adult Protestants characterize themselves as regular in attendance (weekly or almost weekly). Recent Gallup polls are similar to these statistics. Thirty-four percent of the young adults (under age twenty) surveyed rarely or never attend. Twenty-four percent of the young adults attend almost weekly. Fifty-seven percent of those who claim to be Catholic nationwide are women; 63 percent of regular Mass attendees are women.

Other Findings

The Notre Dame study has its own body of data, called the Notre Dame Study of Catholic Parish Life (CPL). This data is based on research in 1,100 parishes, with additional intensive research done in thirty-six parishes. The CPL finds that between one-fourth to one-third of all U.S. Catholics have no parish connections at all. They are so infrequent in church attendance as to be totally unknown by the parish. There are close to 15 million baptized Catholics who have become inactive in their faith. While still claiming to be Catholic, and perhaps maintaining a spiritual life, they have no liturgical or social relationship with a parish. These people are among the many subgroups in a parish, that could be touched by new, creative forms of ministry of reconciliation.

For those who do attend Mass regularly, 80 percent regularly receive communion. As high as 85 percent of young Catholics rarely, or perhaps never experience devotions such as stations of the cross, benediction, public recitation of the rosary, or novenas. People age sixty or over are the most likely to participate in these events.

The Sacrament of Reconciliation

The CPL study distinguishes a group called "core Catholics." Core Catholics are more than culturally Catholic. They have connections with a parish or some other Cath-

olic institution. Among these core Catholics, CPL claims
that 27 percent never go to confession. In its research on
Mass attendance, CPL found that only 5 percent of core
Catholics rarely or never attend Mass and 11 percent rarely
or never commune. Thus, specifically regarding reconciliation, there seems to be core Catholic diffidence. Thirty-
five percent celebrate reconciliation once a year. Thirty-
three percent celebrate several times a year. Five percent
report going to the sacrament once a month. Only 1 percent reported more frequent experience. Among a sub-
group that could be classified as "parish leaders," 15 percent never celebrate the sacrament; 33 percent celebrate
once a year; 44 percent celebrate several times a year;
8 percent confess monthly or even more frequently than
that. The study concludes that while frequency of reconciliation has certainly changed in the last decades, three-
fourths of those connected with a parish experience the
sacrament in some way during the course of a year.

Many who were surveyed for the CPL said that communal reconciliation services were never held at their parishes.
Fifty percent said they never participate in a communal
service. Twenty-nine percent reported doing so twice a
year. Eighteen percent said they participated in such services several times a year. Three percent reported more frequent participation. The CPL reports that some findings
indicate general confusion about the various forms of reconciliation (individual, communal with individual confession and absolution, general absolution) and also about
the legitimacy of other approaches to reconciliation (i.e.,
penitential rite of eucharist, private prayer).

For those who have maintained some devotion to the
sacrament, communal celebrations have not emerged as
the answer to the church's reconciliation problem. Those

who value the sacrament use both the communal service with individual confession and absolution *and* the individual form fairly equally. Others still rely solely on the individual form. Seven percent reported going to communal services, but not confessing. Thirty-one percent go to confession but do not celebrate in communal rituals. Forty-three percent of the core Catholics use both individual and communal formats.

In the thirty-six parishes studied intensively, thirty-one used form II with some frequency. Twenty-seven of the parishes had used form III (general absolution). Three parishes said they used general absolution as the normative way to experience the sacrament. In those parishes that only use general absolution, 41–49 percent of the parishioners never go to private confession. The study opens the following issue up for discussion: do communal services in fact minimize the importance of individual confession, or are these communal offerings the only vehicle many modern Catholics will use to liturgically celebrate reconciliation?

Among the thirty-six parishes under intensive study, thirty-two had weekly individual confession scheduled. All of the parishes said unscheduled individual confessions were both encouraged and easily facilitated. Those most likely to use confession as a means of reconciliation are over sixty years of age. Thirty-eight percent of core Catholics under thirty never go to confession; 37 percent confess once a year; 20 percent confess several times a year; 5 percent confess once a month or more frequently.

Priests' Concerns About Reconciliation

A listening session was held in the Archdiocese of Chicago around the time of the 1983 synod. Most of those in attendance were priests. They spoke of their concern about this dimension of Catholic sacramental life, which to a large extent is their responsibility. While lacking the precision of the GSS and CPL data on lay people's experience with the sacrament, the listening session revealed a similar confusion from a different perspective. The issues reflect well the controversies about reconciliation today. The commentary on each issue is my own.

A) The Sacrament in the Context of Metanoia

Could it be that in its preoccupation with fostering the various rites, some church leaders lose sight of the bigger and perhaps more important issue of *metanoia* and conversion? Conversion, awakening to God, allowing one's self to be progressively transformed by the power of the Spirit, usually involves a similarly progressive turning from sin. People need to be reminded that sacramental reconciliation is one step in a process of turning toward God. Quality catechesis needs to be offered not just on the sacrament as a holy thing that one ought to partake in, but also on the steps on the journey toward reconciliation. Such rounded catechesis should aid people in a contemporary understanding of sin, the nature of adult spirituality and faith, the many types of conversion, and sacraments as rituals of vowing and revowing to the Lord and Kingdom values. The sacrament is not a goal in itself. Rather *conversion that may express itself in a sacramental moment* is the more wholistic focus.

B) Uncertainty About Sin

Not only the ordinary parishioner, but clergy also report confusion about the nature of sin. In our renewed church, perhaps in an over-reaction to our previous preoccupation with guilt, we lean dramatically toward an understanding of and acceptance of the sinner. Such was the style of Jesus. But in our eagerness to share the comfort of Jesus, we must not forget Jesus as challenge. Jesus named and condemned the personal and communal sin of his day. In a similar vein, the church and religious educators need to help disciples develop their ability to *discern sin. Discernment of sin* is quite a bit different from the black and white "naming of sin and doing penance" approach of the tariff penance days. Discernment speaks of watching, waiting, looking, listening, weighing options and consequences, making decisions, taking action, and being willing always to evaluate one's stance and change if it appears to be the moral thing to do.

Discernment speaks of a growing ability to prioritize and value. Discernment of sin cuts through the immature false guilt of preoccupation with religionized sin and sees "the good," "the truth" that we are called to live in a spirit of responsibility, but which we often fail to do. Discerning people are honest about and with themselves and prophetic relative to the culture and world that they live in. We cannot give our young people or ourselves a great deal of black and white in terms of morality. We can, however, advocate principles:

1) *The importance of personal conscience.* No one can give another person a map or a flow chart of rights and wrongs. Each person must search and struggle to form his or her own conscience.

2) *The need for an informed conscience.* Personal conscience can become reckless without formation and guidance. My growing "inner word," needs to be joined to an "outer word," of guidance and authority. A person needs

to critique his or her inner word with the scriptural word of
God, the teaching and tradition of the church, and the wisdom of the sciences. It is the responsibility of pastors, prin-
cipals, and directors of education and their staffs that such
quality information and formation be offered to people.

3) *The value of mentors and soul friends.* Whether a person chooses a priest confessor for this role or not, we all
are in need of being sponsored. As catechumens joining
the church have a friend and guide in the form of the sponsor, each of us needs to have Christian friends who care for
us spiritually. For some, this friendship is found in a base
community, faith-sharing group, or peer ministry group. I
feel that it is often because there is no one with whom to
discuss matters of morality, and to discern the value or dis-
values of a given issue, that many Catholic people, by de-
fault, morally conform to the wisdom of the age.

4) *Responsibility as key to morality.* Theologian Matthew
Fox has written and spoken extensively about the church's
preoccupation with sin since the days of Augustine. Fox's
contention is that we ought to pay more attention to grace
and blessing than to sin. True disciples should be much
more in touch with grace, nature, and beauty than most of
us are. I would like to propose a compromise with Fox's
thought. Let us accept his theological conviction that what
we are and have is grace and blessing. In addition to living
a life of praise for blessing, we need to live in a spirit of responsibility for all that is gift—one's self, one's relationships, one's bond with God, the larger community,
nature, the cosmos, etc. The criterion for morality must
become: "Have I been responsible with my blessings, my
gifts?" Such a question, focused on various dimensions of

human life, is sure to surface much subtle sin, previously ignored or rationalized.

5) *Regular moral inventory.* The Alcoholics Anonymous program encourages its participants to engage in regular moral inventories, discerning the areas of irresponsibility, fault, or woundedness still in need of healing. The theory behind the practice is that it is easy for recovering alcoholics to deflect responsibility for their own lives and sobriety onto others or life if they do not regularly evaluate and direct their own decisions and actions. So also it is with the disciple: We lose that sense of responsibility when we fail to regularly think critically—in a healthy sense— about the direction of our lives.

6) *Personal and Communal Sin.* Too often we have privatized both sin and salvation. Jesus became our personal savior, saving us from our personal sin. While not ignoring personal sin, disciples need to be sensitized to the relational, societal, and global dimensions of sin. Conscience formation needs to involve *conscientizing* relative to the issues of justice in our society and around the world. Liberation theology teaches that to the degree we are not aware of and standing up against social sin, in our complacency, we become the merchants of such sin, the masters of a partially enslaved world. The magisterium's preoccupation with the individual form of the sacrament seems to reenforce privatized sin and to deemphasize the communal nature of sin and forgiveness.

C) Human Sexuality

If the church has had any great preoccupation over many of the past centuries it has been in the area of sex-

uality and sexual sins. This preoccupation has left many
Catholics in past years guilt-ridden or sexually dysfunctional. In *American Catholics Since the Council: An
Unauthorized Report,* Andrew Greeley maintains, from a
foundation of sociological research, that more and more
Catholics are living a kind of "selective Catholicism" in
which they pick and choose which of the church's official
teaching they wish to adhere to or appropriate. While there
is certainly a danger of creating a smorgasbord morality in
such an approach, his research is congruent with my
knowledge of people's experience. Perhaps no area admits
of this selectivism more than human sexuality. I have
known some people whose selectivism has been at variance
with church teaching and their choices and lifestyles have
been, at least apparently, quite moral. On the other hand,
misguided selectivism, frequently in the lives of young
people, has had disastrous results for many.

Whether it is pornographic rock, R-rated movies, or sexual activity, I am not an advocate of hand-slapping or lec-
turing. I am, however, an advocate of discernment. The
doors of sexual awareness and activity that have opened in
America may never be closed again. We need quality time
—as adults for our own well-being and as parents and educators with our young people—to look critically at sexual
mores and questions. Jesus needs to be posed, not as the
answer but rather, as theologian John Shea suggests, as the
question asked of certain values and practices. The key
questions regarding human sexuality are: Does this seem
"of the Lord"? Is this attitude, pattern, habit congruent
with being a disciple? Is this healthy for me and others?

I fear we fail as a church to provide both adults and
young people the environments and situations where
healthy discussion and critical reflection can be applied to

the many issues of human sexuality. To the degree that we fail to dialogue in search of Christian wisdom, the wisdom of the age prevails.

D) The New Reconciliation Rite: Is It Working?

The individual form, encouraged by the magisterium, is not equally relished by the Catholic faithful. I find great benefit personally in my own individual confession of sin and reception of absolution. I also have a quite introverted spirituality. I can equally appreciate, however, forms II and III. There are built-in difficulties with the individual form that I can see as a priest-celebrant. The stages of forms I and II are the same. While praying together, sharing Scripture, praising God together can be quite aesthetically touching in the context of a large group of people, the same steps frequently are experienced as wooden between only two people, priest and penitent. Just as eucharist with only two persons can feel almost uncomfortable at times, so it is with reconciliation.

Private confession can carry with it that privatized notion of sin, while communal services quite obviously locate both sin and forgiveness in the context of community. The individual form frequently is abused by immature people who do not so much want to grow as to relieve pseudo-guilt. Often confessors just process these people through, rather than engaging in therapeutic conversation with them. Are sacraments meant to be private or public experiences? I ask the question both theologically and pragmatically. From the pragmatic viewpoint, will a church that cannot even afford its people regular celebrations of the eucharist in some regions of the world be able to provide priest confessors with much time and expertise in the areas of spiritual direction and one-on-one spiritual healing?

Often the pieces of the individual form are used rather arbitrarily by priests. As a result, people never quite know what to expect. The simultaneous presence of screens and kneelers, with more comfortable chairs for those who want a face-to-face encounter, immediately sends ambiguous, confusing messages to people: Do I stand, kneel, sit? The sharing of Scripture, without the homily offered in the communal form, often seems to be "tacked on." The words of absolution, while reflecting a sound theology of reconciliation, are too verbose and foreign in tone for many penitents. One priest put it well at the listening session: individual confessions seem to fall into two categories: 1) conversion confessions (moments of real *metanoia*) and 2) grocery-list confessions (mechanical listing of sins, hoping the sacrament to do its *ex opere operato* thing).

E) New Words of Absolution for Children?

The revised rite has been criticized for the verbosity and complexity of the words of absolution. This is a special problem in reconciliation with children. Many clergy and religious educators have proposed a shorter, simpler form of absolution that would better communicate to children God's unconditional love and forgiveness.

F) Existential Reconciliation

A young adult asked to see me some time ago to discuss an area of morality that he was concerned about. It included a kind of confession of something about himself that he had concluded was morally wrong. When I asked if he wanted sacramental absolution, he said no. The incident has stayed with me because the time that he spent with me was apparently an experience of reconciliation for him, but he did not want all the trappings of the sacrament. The genuine experience of reconciliation and *metanoia* was more important to him than the ritual celebration of reconciliation. We need always to distinguish the experience of reconciliation from the liturgical celebration of it. The *experience* and the *celebration* need to be equally fostered. Wounded, estranged relationships cannot be healed or swept away with a ritual. Rather they need a process of mutuality and hard work. This theme is echoed in Matthew 18:22, in which Jesus tells Peter to forgive "seventy times seven times"; in Luke 6:27-35, in which Jesus speaks of the necessity of love of enemies, and in numerous other passages. A true experience of the sacrament of reconciliation can be had only if joined to genuine attempts at repairing damaged relationships or working at the integrity and quality of one's own values and attitudes.

If reconciliation is going to be *experienced* by contemporary Catholics, they need not only education about rituals and sacraments, but also in many other dimensions of daily living. Christian parenting skills, marital enrichment, conscientization and politicization about issues of peace and justice, pastoral counseling and spiritual direction, conflict management skills, and many similar activities must become regular offerings at parish gatherings if sacramental reconciliation is to be joined to existential or real reconciliation.

G) Retrieving Penitential, Ascetical Practices

In our renewal efforts over the past twenty years, there are some cases in which we have thrown the baby out with the bath water. One example of this is the decline of penitential practices and asceticism. Perhaps the often neurotic trappings such practices took on in the past had to die before the core value of works of penance could be seen again. Fasting, prayer, almsgiving, and works of self-discipline can all be valuable tools in turning one's mind and heart around, repenting from sin, and/or developing a sense of *solidarity* with victims of injustice, suffering, tragedy, pain, and sickness.

Works of penance need to be encouraged again. But what is needed is "penance with a purpose," that is, penance that is understandable and obviously connected with attempts to grow, raise one's consciousness, or contribute to a renewed social order. "Penance as obligation" often drifted into neurotic guilt-ridden practices. They also made people feel as if they were children, being dictated to by the institution.

"Penance with a purpose," on the other hand, is freely chosen and acted upon. It is an example of real, existential reconciliation. Msgr. John Egan of Chicago, reflecting on the racism present in the neighborhoods of Chicago, said recently: "I used to think that commissions, meetings, and organizations could heal this cancer in our city. I can see now that only prayer and fasting by a number of us can begin to turn some of this around." "Penance with a purpose" is the harnessing of spiritual, emotional energies toward "the good."

H) Reconciliation as a Process

Reconciliation is a process of becoming one, whole, integral—in a person's approach to self, others, the world, and God. In such a process, the ritual, sacramental moment is indeed important. In fact, the process extends across a lifetime, being repeated over and over again. The process of reconciliation, following a catechumenal model, was practiced in the church's early centuries, but it fell into disuse. A contemporary version of such a process might look as follows:

1) *Discernment of sin.* This process was discussed at length earlier in this chapter.

2) *Admission of the need to repent and grow.* Included in this stage is a healthy sense of guilt.

3) *Owning responsibility for one's self, including sin.* Such a stance requires honesty about and with one's self that is often difficult. It also requires a breaking out of a "blaming" syndrome to courageously confront our own shadow side.

4) *Naming our sin.* Rollo May wrote in *Love & Will* that the emotions we fail to identify and name within ourselves often become like demons that control and possess us. But naming them (i.e., jealousy, anger, hurt) places us more congruent with and in control of ourselves. So it is in the area of morality. The sin that we fail to name begins to control us, possess us. We are not really taking hold of ourselves fully if we close our eyes to such a real part of ourselves.

5) *Verbal Sharing.* There is a therapeutic benefit in the verbalizing or sharing of faults with others. Such confession necessitates a kind of humility, a realization that one is not "finished" yet, that one is in need of growth. Verbal confession also seems to prompt a person to want to improve in the area confessed or discussed.

6) *The sacramental encounter.* I use the word "sacramental" in a broad sense here. In this broad sense are included the two connotations of the word *sacrament* that permeate this book: *vow* and *sign.* In terms of vowing, a person in

the process of reconciliation ought to reach a point of resolution in which he/she decides to put aside that which is
hindering the life of discipleship. The flip side of such a
resolution is also a conscious deciding again for Jesus, the
Body of Christ, and discipleship. The reconciling person,
however, also needs a sign, an experience that helps him or
her feel the forgiveness and love of God incarnate in the
here and now. In the rite, absolution ought to be such an
experience. I am suggesting here that for some contemporary Catholics the vow and sign of the sacramental encounter might take the form of something besides absolution.
In the sacramental encounter is also the assurance of divine
help for the sinful area of life, as well as the assurance of
God's mercy.

7) *Therapeutic activity.* If the state of reconciliation is
glimpsed or significantly appropriated, hard work is
needed to maintain such an orientation. Such is at least
one of the functions of penance—to engage in therapeutic
attitudes and activities that reorient the self toward discipleship and help one learn the values and lifestyle of the
disciple. This is the proper function of doing penance.

8) *Beginning of a New Stance.* True reconciliation ought to
lead to a new way of life, though indeed some of the shifts
and changes might be quite small and hardly perceptible.
This new stance includes a renewed outlook on one's self,
one's relationships, and the church community.

The above eight steps speak of a period of time, rather
than a few moments in a confessional or reconciliation
room. Also, this process needs to be joined to the existential reconciliation previously described. Existential reconciliation joined to one's own moral process of reconcilia-

tion constitutes true *metanoia*. These eight steps may or may not involve the sacrament of reconciliation, that is, one of our sacred seven rituals. The ritual of sacramental reconciliation could take on more of a process motif if the various parts of the rite were separated in time (i.e., confession of sin, followed by a period of penance, leading to a later experience of absolution. Such a process could be used in either individual or communal formats.

I) Mixed Reviews for Commual Reconciliation with Individual Absolution

There are indeed mixed feelings about this hybrid style of reconciliation. At the listening session referred to earlier, one priest said that the format was the steady diet of his parish. It is the normative way to celebrate reconciliation in his parish. Others, however, found this format to be schizoid—certainly capturing a communal feeling in the prayer service component, but then privatizing the experience for confession and absolution. Some liturgists complain that the aesthetics and power of the ritual are sacrificed for a rather clumsy maintenance of the individual format of confessing sin and being absolved. The confessing of one sin, often the strategy used to quicken the line of penitents, brings a cold "waiting in line at the store" feeling to the sacred moment. Such insistance on touching bases with the priest again makes the priest the central figure of the celebration.

J) Misusing General Absolution

General absolution is also being abused in some situations. In the name of liberalism and relevancy, makeshift general absolution services are held, as priests "create the need." In some situations, little or no liturgical planning goes into these services, and the focus of attention again becomes the priest's absolution. Too little time is given for a process of reconciliation or to help facilitate the ritual as an expression of what we have called "existential reconciliation."

General absolution—when planned well as part of well-done liturgy—can be a powerful and moving experience. In some situations, like missions and revivals, general absolution, with the opportunity for individual consultation for those who want it, can be a very positive experience of the sacrament. Used in holy seasons like Advent and Lent, it could be a first step in reconciling alienated or inactive Catholics.

K) Sacramental Preparation
with Children, Families, and Adults

I have focused my ministry a great deal on religious education over the past thirteen years. Over the years, I have become more and more convinced of the great potential for evangelization and conversion ministry in the parochial mission of sacramental preparation. I repeat the word *potential,* for most often I feel that parishes do not maximize the potential or opportunity. Sacramental preparation too often becomes a schizoid phenomenon with garbled goals. Too often the focus is on children approaching the sacrament for the first time, and catechesis is given to parents about what is happening to their child. In effect, we often prepare the child for the *holy thing* and explain to the parents the meaning of the holy thing for the child. The end result is that often a child's first experience of reconciliation is his or her last experience until some other event arises, such as preparation for confirmation. In addition, the largely catechetical informational sessions experienced by the parents do little to foster a revaluing of or greater devotion to the sacrament.

One of the great challenges that lie ahead for sacramental preparation and all forms of religious education is a transformation of our "schooling systems" toward a more genuinely evangelizing style of catechesis. I am suggesting that as a church we need to reach for new models: CCD, parochial school, and the current mandatory, instructional sacramental preparation sessions simply are not doing the job. They perpetuate a cultural Catholicism oriented toward the acquiring of holy things but do little to prepare people for sacraments as experiences of vowing or revowing to Jesus, the Kingdom, and the Body of Christ. Below are some principles that I operate out of in coordinating religious education efforts on the parish level. While far from ideal and certainly not effecting "mass conversions," I feel the use of these principles creates more of an environment where conversion or vowing may take place, than in typical sacramental preparation efforts.

1) *From holy things to vows.* If the masses of Catholic people suffer from any one great weakness, it is a lack of awareness of the history of our tradition. Specifically, I fear few Catholics have an adequate understanding of the history and evolution of our sacraments. This lack of understanding and knowledge leads people to the misconception that the style of sacramentalizing that they grew up with is of divine origin and therefore contemporary adaptations are to be resisted. Very few people are aware of the very early connotation of the word *sacramentum,* that is, *vow.* If we as a people were to begin to retrieve the notion of vowing, our sacramental life would have a great deal more impact.

In line with this vowing mentality, educators need to explain baptism as the primordial vow and all other sacraments as a re-echoing of that first vow. Avery Dulles, in *A Church to Believe In,* suggests that our sacramental system be reinterpreted around the theological notion of *discipleship.* He is speaking of the same idea that I have shared. Baptism is our first vow to begin a life of discipleship. Reconciliation is the experience of being forgiven and then re-vowing after one's initial vow has been negatively affected by sin.

2) *Teaching on the meaning of conversion.* Too many Catholics, even in this post-Vatican II age, still think of *conversion* as the changing of denominations, i.e., a Protestant becoming Catholic. We need to break open for the wide body of believers the scriptural understanding of conversion, namely, an awakening to God incarnate in human experience and a progressive process of turning from sin and illusion to God and peace. Across the whole sacramental spectrum, it is the reception of *holy things* without conversion of life that robs sacraments of power and renders them vehicles of cheap grace.

3) *Education as socialization.* The stories of Scripture and the tradition of our church can only be successfully transmitted through an education that includes socialization. Religious educators Thomas Groome, John Westehoff, Parker Palmer, and others, have written and spoken extensively about how the "religion as subject-schooling model" of religious education will continue to produce diminishing results if not joined to religious socialization. Reconciliation, either as existential behavior in relationships or as sacramental ritual, will not be valued by young people if they are not being socialized into an adult com-

munity that values existential and sacramental reconciliation. Education and socialization relative to reconciliation require that children and parents *together* creatively and experientially appropriate and reappropriate all that we mean by reconciliation.

Family education means more than mandating parents to attend a few, often irrelevant and boring, theological sessions in the church auditorium. It means that in practical ways families (including single parent families) together, in a progressive way, be led to understand and appreciate the values of reconciling and celebrating, recognizing and discerning personal and social sin. In short, I feel it is important for parents to celebrate the sacrament *with* their children on the occasion of the first celebration. Afterward, the parish ought to offer regular, small-group reconciliation services for families, according to the children's developmental level. It ought to be understood that participation in such religious experiences with one's children is as important as catechetical sessions.

4) *A catechumenal model.* In stylizing curricula for sacramental preparation, I try to include a journey motif for each sacramental program. Such a strategy attempts to begin sacramental preparation by speaking to the participants' needs, questions, or hurts, as well as by the formation of relationships among the members of the group and a primary proclamation of Jesus and his vision. This evangelization stage then leads to a period of catechesis, for example, sessions on the history and contemporary meaning of reconciliation. Catechesis flows into a period that parallels the catechumens' election period, or period of close, proximate preparation for the sacramental celebration. The sacrament—specifically reconciliation—is celebrated as a revowing to the meaning of one's baptism. The

celebration is not an end in itself but rather becomes the beginning of a new stance toward the Lord and the Christian community.

While not all the sacramental preparation programs I coordinate follow this description perfectly, I have tried to adapt the same process for preparation for baptism, reconciliation, confirmation, eucharist, and marriage. In each of the sacramental preparation programs, candidates celebrate the achieving of certain plateaus in the presence of the Sunday assembly. This happens with some regularity. This interaction with the Sunday congregation reminds both the candidates and their families of the communal nature of sacraments, as well as challenging the congregation to appreciate the particular sacrament. While the Holy Spirit, not the ministers, is the agent of conversion, the ministers nonetheless are responsible for creating an environment where conversion is facilitated.

Many American parishes have ignored the Vatican's admonition and retained first reconciliation where they had experimentally placed it some years before—in fourth or fifth grade. It was the thinking at the time that children are intellectually, emotionally, and morally more capable of understanding sin, forgiveness, and reconciliation in intermediate grades than at age seven. Other parishes, in obedience to the Vatican's request, immediately moved the sacrament back to second grade, preceding first communion.

Would it not be to the advantage of all concerned to see catechesis about reconciliation as a process that extends over many years—introducing young children to prayer services and liturgies of the Word, later grades to communal services with individual absolution, intermediate grades to general absolution and good experiences of the individual format? Again, in each preparation effort, the approach should be family-based and catechumenal in nature. After an initial "progressive entrance into reconciliation," additional catechesis should be available to promote existential and sacramental reconciliation for all the developmental stages from childhood on.

5) *Beware of legalism.* While the foregoing approach to sacramental preparation might appear a bit stringent and disciplined, I try to never encase it in legalistic wrappings. I feel it is possible to communicate expectations to people without simultaneously sounding legalistic or punitive. If people cannot, for some good reason, be part of a communal preparation effort, provisions must always be made for exceptions. In addition, expectations should always be explained from a view of the value of the expectations for the qualitative and integral experience of the sacrament. Many clergy and religious educators do "counter-evangelization" in making preparation for reconciliation and other sacraments appear to be a series of hoops that individuals, couples, or families must jump through if they are to receive the prize—the sacrament.

6) *Discernment of readiness.* In the golden era of the catechumenate, preparation for the sacraments of initiation required a variety of ministries. No priest or catechetical director coordinated the whole effort. Rather, different people, members of the Body of Christ, participated in the formation of candidates for the sacraments according to their gifts and charisms. A significant participant in this process was the *sponsor,* who served as a kind of *soul-friend* or *mentor* during the movement toward sacramental celebration. Perhaps in our multiplication of parish ministries, one that we ought to consider reactivating, not just for catechumens, but also for candidates and their families for all sacraments is the role of sponsor. To counteract the

toxic, rigid thinking that dictates "there's a certain time or age" to celebrate a sacrament, the sponsor could act as an agent of discernment helping candidates and families to recognize whether they really are ready for vowing or revowing and if genuine conversion and repentance are being celebrated in the sacrament. Such discernment would in no way be intended as punitive, but rather an attempt to add integrity and truth to the sacramental celebration, in the hope that the sacrament might truly celebrate something real in a person's life.

7) *Dismissals and Follow-up.* "Thanks be to God," the congregation responds when the celebrant announces "the Mass is ended!" The woodenness of the English does not carry a nuance of meaning from earlier Latin forms. The dismissal at Mass and at each sacrament is a commissioning, a sending forth. Dismissals, executed properly, reorient the community from the special, mythic time of liturgy to the real time of everyday living in the marketplace. Sacraments are not ends in themselves. Rather they celebrate growth having taken place and send participants forth to live the growth, grace, and conversion that has been experienced and celebrated. Tad Guzie says it well in his *Book of Sacramental Basics:* there ought to be a new stance toward God, others, life, and community as a result of the process of sacramental preparation and celebration. The moment of dismissal is a brief verbal statement of what ought to be clear through the sacramental process: the end of the sacramental ritual is really the beginning of something new.

In our style of doing sacraments we "leave the evangelical back door open." The staff and religious educators relate to those who have celebrated sacraments as if something has been completed, terminated. So, often after first celebrations (eucharist, reconciliation) there is not a second, third, or fourth, for some time. People come in the front door through the sacrament and rather quickly pass out the back door to inactivity and non-participation. As catechumens experience a *mystagogia,* or a final period of formation following the celebration of the sacrament, so also all people who have journeyed toward a sacrament need ministry that follows up, continues nurturance, and helps an individual or family find a new place in the community. This speaks again of the need for development of a variety of ministries, besides those of education and celebration, to help in the *accompaniment* or sponsoring of candidates.

Having considered principles for sacramental preparation in general, we now focus specifically on reconciliation.

L) Communities of Meaning and Healing

The style of ministry performed by Jesus was a simple one. The Scriptures reveal that he taught; after he taught he healed. Speaking the word of meaning encapsuled in his Kingdom teaching quite often was joined to a touch that healed. A recurrent theme of this book has been that the church and parish have a mandate from the Lord to be agents of reconciliation. We cannot allow ourselves to think narrowly, to think that "all that reconciliation is" is contained in the sacrament. The sacrament of reconciliation is one very special instrument in the larger context of the church's responsibility to reconcile. One area in which this reconciliation ought to be carried out is that of healing ministries.

Pollster George Gallup recently announced his finding that many Catholics wish the local parish would offer op-

portunities for pastoral counseling. Joining the skills of the
psychotherapist to spiritual direction skills, the pastoral
counselor brings the healing power of faith to bear on
problems. Some parishes around the country are setting
aside budget and office space to attend to this important
dimension of the church's responsibility to reconcile. Related to pastoral counseling, more and more people are
seeking spiritual direction, not just guidance for problems,
but for living a life of reconciliation.

The charismatic renewal movement has reminded all of
us of the healing power of prayer. In liturgy, teaching,
preaching, and ministry, parishes ought to remind disciples
of the great power for healing available to each of us spontaneously. The power of prayer at times exorcises and
heals when other tools fail. A noted priest, a spiritual
director in Chicago, has a specialized ministry for women
feeling guilty and depressed over abortions they have had.
Prayerfully, this priest leads women back to the months of
pregnancy; he encourages them to give a name to the
aborted fetus and then to address both God and the fetus,
seeking forgiveness and reconciliation. The experience is
powerfully reconciling for those who have experienced it,
much more so than something that might take place in a
cold, austere confessional.

Besides pastoral counseling, spiritual direction, and
healing prayer, other dimensions of the parish's responsibility to reconcile include the many healing ministries that
a contemporary parish needs. Among the many subgroups
crying out for healing ministries are: the divorced and
separated; the widowed or those grieving; the addicted; the
families of the addicted; the unemployed; those in need of
help in coping with anxiety, stress, and depression; the
sick; the terminally ill; and many others. Through the

development of peer to peer ministries and creative programs, the local church can facilitate much "existential reconciliation."

The international evangelical youth movement, Youth for Christ, has an approach to youth ministry from which our church could learn a great deal. Their youth ministry operates on two tracks. The first track is for the relatively healthly young people dealing with the crises of adolescence. Through social events, retreats, and religious education, the ministers progressively lead the young people toward a discovery of Jesus as source of meaning and creative influence in their lives. Track two is for troubled young people—those with identity or relational problems, those estranged from family, friends, institution, or society. The stated goal of their "ministry to troubled youth" is *reconciliation*. Through counseling and spiritual direction, adult and peer ministers attempt to lead troubled young people to reconciliation: with themselves, with significant others, with society, and with God and the Body of Christ.

As with parish-based pastoral counseling, so also ministry to troubled youth is virgin territory for most Catholic parishes. Even if individual parishes would find pastoral counseling, spiritual direction, and ministry to troubled youth financially impossible, such ministries of reconciliation could be done well regionally, with parishes pooling resources for the hiring of adequate personnel.

M) Reconciliation and the Inactive Member

Much of my work over the past few years has focused on the inactive Catholic. As the Notre Dame study indicated, one-fourth to one-third of most parishes' potential congregation have no contact at all with their local parish. It is

my own speculation that another third are only tenuously
attached to their parish. Up to two-thirds of many
parishes' congregations are estranged from the community. Thomas Sweetser, of the Parish Evaluation Project in
Chicago, says that of the people who are regular in church
attendance, approximately 90 percent are "active-unin-
volved"; that is, the relationship is largely liturgical in
nature. They are not actively involved in parish organizations or ministries.

In another book, *The Evangelizing Parish,* I discuss in
detail the reasons for alienation from the church, as well as
programatic suggestions on how to reach out to them. I
wish to share in this book only a few ideas on this topic.
First of all, I will share a principle: People are not returned
to church by people trying to get them back to church.
People may return to active membership if a number of life
situations push them in that direction and if they meet or
are aware of a local community that communicates care
and concern for them. What is needed in parishes is not
"get them back to church" programs, but rather ministries
of care and reconciliation. Concern for the inactive member is an extension of the parish's ongoing pastoral care.
Behind the reasons and issues often given for becoming
inactive, there are often painful life issues that become
connected with nonchurch attendance. The parish must
communicate concern for those real life issues that are a
cause of pain and estrangement.

Some strategies that my research and experience have
shown to be effective in reaching out to the inactive member are:

1) the training of calling teams to regularly visit all pa-
   rishoners, active and inactive: to listen to needs, nur-

ture active members, and begin reconciliation with inactive ones;

2) needs-based adult education that addresses real issues in the personal, familial, and business worlds of the community;

3) improved sacramental preparation which gives ample time to parishioners' questions of faith, the formation of relationships, and discernment of readiness for sacraments;

4) extensive ministry of care to the sick in homes and hospitals;

5) mini-catechumenal series that provide opportunities for those who want to return to update themselves.

These are only several suggestions. There are many, many more possibilities for building bridges of reconciliation to the inactive member. Inactive Catholics need time to talk, good relationships with church members, new faith experiences, and new information about the church.

N) Reconciliation and Social Justice

Conversion is incomplete when the only focus is the self and God. Personal conversion finds completion in sharing in the mission of social conversion or change. "Would that all of God's people would be prophets," Moses says to Joshua in the Book of Numbers (11:28). To be prophetic is, through both activity and resistance, to attempt to reconcile the world to God in our small piece of time and history. Jim Wallis writes prophetically in the *Call to Conversion* that too many Christians are "spiritually lukewarm" and "politically conforming." We allow the world

to pass us by rather than reshaping the world. Through
preaching, religious education, and parish ministries, the
local church needs to be in a constant stance of *conscientization* (raising consciousness about the values of the Kingdom and how they critique society), and *politicization* (in
often small but real ways taking action for the seamless
garment of justice and respect for life).

O) An Ecumenical Perspective

Not only the Roman Catholic Church but also other
Christian bodies have turned attention to reconciliation in
recent years. The revised Anglican *Book of Common
Prayer* and the revised *Lutheran Book of Worship* both include rites of reconciliation. While baptism and eucharist
are emphasized as the primary sacraments, reconciliation is
nonetheless included as among the churches' rites and sacraments. All three of the revised rituals (Anglican, Lutheran, and Catholic) contain the same major ritualistic
steps of welcoming the penitent: use of Scripture, confession of sins to the appropriate minister, prayer of sorrow,
words of absolution, and dismissal. The theology behind
all three revised rituals stresses the communal nature of
both sin and reconciliation, and the sacrament of reconciliation's connection with baptism.

P) Confessions of Devotion

A lingering question is the value and importance of confessions of devotion, or regular experiences of sacramental
reconciliation. If the sacrament is frequented as part of a
regular, healthy moral inventory, then such practices
should be encouraged and supported by ministers. On the
other hand, if confessors perceive that regular confession
is part of a neurotic compulsion, a poorly formed cons-

cience, or a problematic God-image, those priests have a responsibility to gently begin guidance and reeducation for these troubled people.

Something that troubles me about sacramental practice around the country is that the parishes with the longest individual confession and absolution lines are frequently the parishes where no catechesis or updating has been done relative to sin and the sacrament. The spiritual and moral immaturity of some of those confessing is reinforced, rather than an alternate vision and approach to the sacrament being presented. As some of the developmental theorists have shown, a person can never be forced to move to another stage of moral development. But by at least presenting alternate frames of reference we can open a door of potential growth to some people in need of it.

Discussion Questions

1. What is the relationship between real-life reconciliation and sacramental reconciliation?
2. The community (parish) has a responsibility for a very broad and varied ministry of reconciliation. Discuss.
3. Some people ought to be discouraged from celebrating reconciliation, for they are misusing the sacrament. Discuss.
4. How often ought an adult Catholic celebrate reconciliation?

Suggested Readings

Andrew Greeley, *American Catholics Since the Council: An Unauthorized Report*
Tad Guzie, *The Book of Sacramental Basics*
Clark Hyde, *To Declare God's Forgiveness*
Theodore Issac Rubin, *Reconciliation: Inner Peace in an Age of Anxiety*
Jim Wallis, *The Call to Conversion*

An Evangelical Postscript

This book has focused a great deal on history, practical suggestions, and challenges awaiting us in the future. Perhaps our greatest challenge is to *evangelize* our Catholic people. Morality will flow from evangelization and conversion. To analyze moral decision making and conscience formation without a concern also for evangelization is to place too much emphasis on one end of the continuum. Evangelization is the primary stage on that continuum that leads to moral conversion and a reconciled life. Specifically, we who are concerned with moral education and a renewed appreciation of reconciliation, need to lead people to an experience of Jesus, his vision, his story. We need to proclaim the person, the vision, and the story of Jesus, so that it is heard amid the many other stories and value systems that crowd contemporary believers' lives and minds. A heartfelt acceptance of Jesus as Lord, a life-long series of decisions for him, an appropriation of his values, leads to a moral, reconciled life.

Perhaps we have spent too much time teaching the *what* and the *how,* the skills of conscience and morality, and not enough time on the *why,* that is the person, vision, and story of Jesus. In a word, the Kingdom of God is, at least in part, a way of *perceiving.* The nature of the perception is to see, feel, decide, and judge as Jesus would. Sin will always be a part of each of our lives, but evangelized people always want to reach for "the good," because they have met the Rabbi; and they want to continue on the journey of discipleship. Discipleship involves always being in a posture of appropriating the Lord's values, and continuing his mission of meaning and healing.

111